A Girl Named Truth
a memoir

Alethea Kehas

Cover Design: Kelsey Hunt

Library of Congress Cataloging-in-Publication Data

Kehas, Alethea

A Girl Named Truth

Alethea Kehas

p. cm.

ISBN: 978-0-692-92157-9

Library of Congress Control Number: 2017912310

U.S.A

For my families of four

Opal Truth
(after e.e. cummings)

look for my truth my opal
truth with a blue fire in it
you can (love me) still

reach for the ember the cold
ember with old ash on it
(love me) you can still

taste it with a soft tongue
soft with a new silk on it
you can still (love me

deep in your truth in
your truth in truth
now) love me (still)

Contents

Author's Note

This memoir contains memories that have shaped my truth, however altered they may be by time and my own perception. Added to these memories are the stories told to me by those who were willing to share, in part, some of their own truths. Photographs open each chapter, offering a stilled moment of time captured by an unseen photographer. Yet even these are subject to the truths of the artist and the hands of their keepers. The poems that follow the photographs share another rendition of truth. They are erasure poems; words pulled from the chapters they preface. Everything you will see and read is truth in some form.

Truth

open the room of my mind

search for me
within faded

doubt
listen to words
sing

My birth
There was once a girl named
Alethea

her heart sparked with truth

My mother told me she found my name, Alethea, in a book. In my child-mind I created a tome perfumed with age, adding gilded pages over the years. Sometimes I imagined stories, filled with strong and beautiful goddesses, and smiled with the thought that I was held inside pages I had never read.

"It's Greek," my mother told me, "for truth."

When I opened the book inside the room of my mind, I watched the pages unfold like the wings of a butterfly, and waited for a girl named truth to manifest into form.

I never doubted the origin of my name, until one winter afternoon when I was thirty-six. That day, alone in my New Hampshire home, I cupped a phone to my ear and listened to my father's words as he spoke from three thousand miles away inside a small ivory bungalow on the coast of Washington state.

"Did I ever tell you where your name came from?" he asked.

"No," I said, my heart beginning to race his words. "I always thought it came from a book."

My father's nervous chuckle mixed with his words. "No, we got the idea from a TV show. Your mother and I used to watch a series called 'Kung Fu' together," he said with another soft laugh that sounded almost like an apology. "It was popular in the 70s. There was an episode with a little girl named Alethea the year you were born."

I scoured the drawers of the coffee table for a pencil and a pad of paper to record my father's words, while my heart searched for a steady rhythm. This was not the same truth I had clung to all these years. The tome I had held close to my heart was beginning to disintegrate with the words of my father.

Later, after I hung up the phone, I Googled the episode my father had referenced. The words on the screen shifted me into another reality: " 'Kung Fu' Alethea, 1973." I clicked the YouTube link below the image and prepared to watch and listen.

Against a backdrop of daisies, the name Alethea appeared in orange ink, followed by Jodi Foster as a young girl plucking the strings of a mandolin atop a rocky cliff. I watched the spunky blonde actress I had always admired, boldly follow the stranger she had just met, the traveling Shaolin priest Caine, played by David Carradine.

"They call me Leethe," she told him as she extended her hand in greeting, "but my real name is Miss Alethea Patricia Abrahams."

My mind traveled back in time thirty years to when my paternal grandmother, Grammie, used to call me Leethe.

She could almost be me, I thought as I watched Jodi Foster, if my hair had been lighter and I had been a child with courage. Here before me was a girl who seemed to live without fear, yet we both shared the burden of a name that meant "truth." Neither of us could escape the weight of what it stood for.

Like the fictional Alethea, I struggled with the concept of truth. As a young child, if I told a lie, which was not often, I thought of my name. When I detected someone else's lie, I thought of my name. Alethea. It was my anchor, it was my legacy, and it was my compass. Now my name was guiding me through the stormy seas of my past, as I tried to redefine myself against the truths I was raised on.

I heard the words of the falsely imprisoned Caine reassure the young Alethea, "Do not condemn yourself for telling the truth," while men outside the building banged nails into the gallows being built to hang him.

My mind swirled back into the past, remembering a childhood lived inside the shadows of secrets and truths I didn't want to believe, before I heard Caine's voice again, "Each step we take is built on what has gone before." I watched as the character Alethea discovered how truth is often a matter of perception, and can be clouded by emotions and fears.

"The people of Greece have a name for truth," Caine's words rang clear and strong. "Alethea. Alethea is a girl who loves the truth."

As Caine disappeared down the dusty road toward his next adventure, Alethea became a girl with light-brown hair and dark-blue eyes shadowed by distrust; a girl who created a shield of her mother's words, blocking out her inner truth.

I thought of the stories my mother had told me of a life before I was old enough to remember it, and began to compare them to the new stories I was receiving from my father. In so many ways, they did not fit together, and I now tried to imagine my parents before my mother decided she hated my father. They must have been happy, I realized, for at least a little while.

Instead of a sad young woman with long, brown braids sitting on an old tapestried couch reading a book against her swollen belly with my one-year-old sister, Tara, clung beside her, I saw a family of three gathered on a sofa, watching a small TV perched atop a wooden crate. I even allowed my parents to touch hands and smile as they looked into each other's eyes and shared the same thought, *Alethea, we'll name our child Alethea, if she is another girl. For truth.*

Father

deliver
me
home

father
wrap
my
body

hold me
"Daddy"

In the
River time

wash away

omission

I was the second of two unplanned pregnancies. My parents conceived my sister in the spring of 1971. My mother was barely nineteen, my father who was halfway through college, was twenty-years-old. After they realized they had a baby on the way, my parents got married in a civil ceremony, and my father dropped out of school to get a job.

My sister Tara was born at the "County Hospital" in Portland, Oregon. "It was my only option," my mother told me, "because I was poor." No family or friends were permitted in the birthing room, and Tara was born into the cold hands of strangers. The nurses, in their eagerness to get my mother up and walking after the delivery, refused to wait for the numbness of the medication to leave her body. Instead, they slammed her legs over the side of the bed, then released her. The legs that could not yet support her collapsed my mother into a heap on the hard floor below. "I wasn't going to repeat that horrible experience," my mother told me, "so I had you at home."

Nineteen months later, shortly after one o'clock on the last Thursday in August, I was born with the aid of a chiropractic doctor in my parents' bedroom. "He was a kind man," my mother told me.

After I left my mother's body, the doctor delivered me into the hands of my maternal grandmother, who bathed me clean of the sticky fluids of my mother's womb in a warm basin of soapy water. Where my father was during my delivery was never shared with me, so I imagined him pacing the hallway outside his bedroom door while my mother labored inside. In my childhood fantasy, he waits until I am pushed free of my mother's body, cleaned, and wrapped loosely in a blanket. Only then is he allowed to enter the room where my grandmother places his eight-and-a-half pound baby girl on his lap.

After my grandmother's hands release me, I see the white blanket fall with gravity against my father's legs, revealing to him for the first time, my naked form. I imagine his face as it peered into mine. His eyes recognize first what we share, making his lips curl toward a smile. The frown follows quickly, though, as he lingers on the part that is wrong.

My father wanted me to be a boy. He had been so convinced I would be a boy, in fact, that he chose the name Eamon, and insisted upon keeping it for my middle name after I was born. "Like a joke," my mother told me when I was a child, her voice laced with animosity. I grew to hate this middle name, which I thought of as an ugly, cruel gift from a father who never wanted me.

Years later, the scenes harbored in my mind began to change as I examined thirty-three photographs my father had sent to me. I saw his arms hold me in two of them, and when I turned their images over, I read a name I can't remember saying, "Daddy."

I don't know how many times my eyes studied the blurred face peering into my infant form in their search for connection. My mind, I know, struggled to retrieve memories that it had not kept. To find the recognition of a father when I saw only a stranger who looked a lot like me. Yet, there were blessings to what I could not find. Nowhere in my father's young face did I read anger or rejection. Instead I read sadness, and the faint lines of love.

After the photographs, my father began sending me letters and other documents he had saved from the early years of my life. With his written words I was able to discover a part of a man I never really knew. In letters to his mother, I read of a father's hope for his young family before it was taken away from him.

In the fall of 1974, when I was a year old, my parents decided to abandon the comforts of modern life, and took the four of us to southern Oregon to live like hippies. Our departure was sudden and mysterious, my parents telling their families that they were taking us to camp along the Clackamas River. We didn't appear back in Portland for several months, and in that time away my mother stopped loving my father.

We set up camp in Kerby, an old mining town at the southern tip of Oregon. Weeks later we moved to a crude A-frame cabin beside the river in Cave Junction. There was no electricity or plumbing inside our home, which was downstream from a commune that used the river for washing human waste away. As a result, my father developed a staph infection that made him very ill. My sister and I, who took sponge baths, were somehow spared. My father told me this on the phone thirty-five years later, and there is no mention of his illness in the letters he sent home to his mother.

Instead, my father's written words are almost stubbornly optimistic. In one of the first letters, he begins with this statement, "Well we made it and is it ever beautiful."

"Dear Mother," he writes days later. "I am writing this letter in the hope that it will bring just a little more understanding between us all." The words that grab me most, though, are at the bottom of the second page, "It is hard for me to say everything that I feel at one time, but Diana is not leading me around and I have my feelings on how the two of us live and relate to each other."

My father's words continue on to say how he does not want my mother to have a "traditional role" of the suppressed wife. "I don't know if this makes any sense to you but I get the impression that both you and Diana's parents get the impression that she is running the whole operation," he writes to his mother. "Whatever we do, it is out of love and respect for each other and done cooperatively."

These words tell a different truth than the stories my mother told me as a child. Reading his written words, I can now believe my father loved and respected my mother, and cared about me and Tara as his daughters.

What he leaves out of his correspondence reveals as much to me as what my father includes. Perhaps most significant, is the omission of the visit we had from Keith while we were living in Cave Junction. Keith, a relative of my mother's, had traveled across the country with a friend on motorcycles, and stopped by to visit with us before he headed back east. During that visit, I believe, Keith and my mother fell in love. Weeks later, when we returned to Portland, we were no longer living with my father as a family of four.

In my earliest memory we are back in Portland, and I am visiting my father who is now living with his mother. I can still recall Grammie's plaid sofa where I sat with my cousin Laura and Tara. A framed print of Sir Walter Firle's "The Fairy Tale" hangs above our heads. The idyllic image of three cherubic girls sitting on a couch reading a book together in the sunshine draws me in. It is like we are the girls in the picture, only I am not happy. I cannot concentrate on the story Laura is reading us, instead my thoughts are running to save my mother.

Grammie's living room is dark and filled with shadows. I can hear my parents, and their voices are loud and angry. I am worried my father is going to hurt my mother. I think I can hear their footsteps, and don't realize it's my own heart pounding inside my chest, like a bird in a cage trying to be free. I am sure my father is chasing my mother. In my two-year-old mind I see her falling because he has pushed her. I want to run to her, to save her, but my body won't move.

"It's okay," Laura whispers, as she cups my knee. "Everything is going to be okay."

I don't believe her. My mother needs me, and I want to help her, but Laura's hand is a brick, and my body is ice. I can barely breathe. When, finally, my mother comes into the room to take us home, I wrap her legs, and watch the early bloom of a bruise on the soft skin above me.

This is the only memory I have kept of my father before we moved to New Hampshire and left him behind when I was four-and-a-half years old. It took me thirty-three years to ask my mother, indirectly, about that day at Grammie's.

"Was he ever physically abusive to you?" I asked in the semi-private space of my home office. During the pause between my question and my mother's answer, I could almost hear my stepfather breathing through the grate that opens the floor to the living room below.

"Once, only once he pushed me around," my mother said. I had no reason to doubt her words, my body knew where her memory would take us.

As I listened to my mother, I began to shake. Only the details of her story varied with the one I had held wrapped inside of me. My mother's remembered scene of violence took place on Grammie's front lawn, while I had imagined the climactic moment occurring inside of the bathroom. This is what memory does; it reshapes over time, like an amoeba searching for solid form. It's slippery, elusive, and subject to change. It clings to hopes and fears when it resurfaces. As a young child, bathrooms were sources of insecurity and fear for me. It only makes sense that I placed my mother, on that fateful day, in the bathroom.

While my mother spoke, I saw her transform into a young woman with long hair hanging like brown curtains against her chest. I saw my father enter the scene with a face free of lines, but not without anger, and watched him as he grabbed, with force, the woman who was still his wife. His motive for rage, though, eluded me. "For some reason he was upset with me and didn't want me to take you girls home," my mother said. Why, I wondered, but did not ask, would the father my mother always told us only cared about himself, not want his daughters to leave?

As I listened to my mother relive her frustration and anger, I relived my fear. My chest compressed my breath, and my legs vibrated involuntarily against my seat. My body, I realized while I tried unsuccessfully to control it, had stored fear into its cells along with the need to save my mother. I was feeling the beat of its fists, once again, as it pounded for release.

Clear my life

pierce a
landscape of water filling
Tulsi, cut free
memory
my fingers
abandon me to birth
harmony
Krishna
dress me in
black curls my body is
blue. I wear a
wrap of
the child
I remember

Shortly after I formed my first memory, my mother ran away with me and Tara to go into hiding with the Hare Krishnas. We left soon after my sister turned four-years-old, in the year 1976. In a photograph taken at her birthday celebration at my maternal grandparents', Tara wears an almost forced look of exuberance on her face. Her body bisects my mother's and father's as we gather near the cake. My mother smiles with her arms around me and her youngest brother, while my father and I look serious and a little unsure.

In the photograph, there are no visible signs of the turmoil my mother later shared in the stories she told me when I was a child. There is no evidence of a family refusing to help her, or of a villainous husband who stole into his house when his family was not home to rummage through what he was asked to leave behind.

Did my mother, I wonder, know she was going to leave on the day of Tara's birthday? For in a matter of weeks, at the most, we had disappeared. We left our home in Portland in secret. My mother discretely packed a large cloth bag with clothes and shoes for three, hoisted its weight upon her back, gathered me and Tara, and boarded a bus to Seattle. In Seattle my mother joined a Hare Krishnas commune, who offered us shelter and food in return for her welfare check.

While we were in Seattle, my mother had our heads shaved so we would no longer look like girls, even though our ears were pierced and beads of Tulsi were strung around our necks. We stayed in Seattle for six weeks; just long enough for my mother to find a sense of community, but not long enough for us to be found.

Soon after we left Portland, my extended family began searching for us. While my maternal grandmother made phone calls, my father hired a private investigator and quit his job. They were not

15

surprised to discover we had run away with the Hare Krishnas, a group that my mother had become involved with before she separated from my father. "I blame the Hare Krishnas," my grandmother says when she talks about my childhood and her own relationship troubles with my mother. "That's when it all started," she tells me. Yet sometimes she also talks about God and how he gave us free-will, and about my mother when she was a teen, holding up her hand and saying as she left the room, "keep talking, I'm not listening."

"I wish we would have helped your mother more," my grandmother also confesses. "But we had a lot going on, especially with George [one of my mother's younger brothers] who was getting into a lot of trouble at the time." Perhaps, though, they had also reached the point of frustration with a daughter for whom they had bought a house, then sold it to buy her a bigger one, as her family grew. A daughter who, weeks after she moved into the second home, abandoned it to live as a hippie in southern Oregon. This was not the first time she had left her family without word of where she was going.

While my grandmother made her phone calls and prayed for our return, my father got into his brown Ford truck and headed up to Washington state, hoping to find us before we left. He was too late. We were already on a bus traveling south. When he discovered we had left the Hare Krishna temple in Seattle, my father tried his luck in Canada. The road to Canada proved to be a long detour, and in Vancouver, my father discovered we had joined the Hare Krishna commune in San Diego.

In San Diego, my mother was happy for a while. She told me here "the food was good, and the people were caring. There were also many women like my mother with young children. Mothers who are all poor and trying to hide from the lives they have chosen to leave behind. We stayed in San Diego for four months, and to

16

help us learn about our new world, Tara and I were given comic books filled with tales of the Hindu gods.

When my father arrived by plane in San Diego, we had been missing for six months. The dates on his rental car receipts, saved all these years, read "July 1976." In San Diego, my father enlisted the help of my mother's only sister, Jane, who was living in San Diego, but had not been aware we were there. Together my father and aunt created a plan, and late one night they carried it out.

Jane drove the rented VW to the Hare Krishna compound in San Diego, and parked outside the building where devotees of Krishna slept. She waited in darkness while my father crept to the nearest window, slowly raised its glass and slipped inside. Without waking the resting bodies, my father peered through the gray light in search of three sets of shoes. Two small pairs, and one large enough to fit a grown woman. He left without luck. Once again, he was too late. My mother, having already been alerted that he was on his way to find us, had boarded a plane with me and Tara bound for West Virginia.

Before my father discovered we were gone, he took a break to body surf in the cool waves of the Pacific Ocean. Bad fortune met him in the form of another surfer, who crashed into him, leaving my father with bruises and broken ribs. Despite his injuries, my father made his way to a Hare Krishna festival the next day, and searched through the sea of faces for the three he had lost. Too broken to continue after not finding us in the crowd, my father decided to return to Portland.

In a letter that he saved and sent to me many years later, along with his rental car receipts, my father wrote the following words: "I am trying to find my two daughters, Tara (4) and Alethea (2), who are with their mother. I have just been granted legal custody of the children and I am trying everything I can to locate them and bring

17

them home. They have been living with the Hare Krishna people in San Diego and were receiving public assistance there. When I found out their whereabouts I flew to San Diego but as soon as they found out I was there the Krishna people moved them to some other unknown place. These people refuse to give any information and will do whatever is necessary to hide people."

What my father didn't know was that we were now living in West Virginia, where an opulent golden palace was being built for the god Krishna and his devotees. The Hare Krishna commune in West Virginia was not filled with kindness, like in San Diego. The meager meals of nutritionally unbalanced meals bloated our bellies, and turned our skin ashen. The people in charge, according to my mother, were "hard core, and all for the cause." When I asked for more details about what our lives were like living with the Hare Krishsnas, especially for Tara and me, my mother told me, "I don't want to talk about it."

While we were in San Diego and in West Virginia, my maternal grandmother continued to make phone calls to try to find us. She enlisted the help of a friendly operator who agreed to dial the numbers of each Hare Krishna establishment that was listed. During one call, my grandmother was almost certain she heard her daughter's voice. With each phone call, she became increasingly frustrated that my mother did not want to be found. When my grandmother discovered that we had relocated to West Virginia, that all three of our names had been changed, and that Tara and I were now living disguised as boys, my grandmother nearly gave up hope.

Each night before she went to sleep, my grandmother kneeled on the green carpet of her bedroom and prayed to God to bring us home. One morning, after we had been missing for nearly eight months, a man approached my grandmother with a pile of mail. As he drew near, she recognized him as the reverend who had bought

18

their old home. He had come to deliver a stack of letters addressed to the former inhabitants.

"How are you doing?" he asked my grandmother after she told him about her missing daughter and granddaughters.

"I pray for them every night," she replied.

"How are you praying?" he asked.

"I ask God to make my daughter come to her senses and come home," she confessed.

"You are praying the wrong way," the reverend replied not unkindly. "God gave us all free will, you must ask Him to inspire your daughter to come home."

Days later, my mother called my grandmother from a hotel in New York, and told her that she had escaped with me and Tara from the Hare Krishna compound in West Virginia. My grandmother listened to her daughter as she told her about a friend who had helped us sneak out of the building, undetected, in the middle of the night, and of the kind dentist who, with his wife, retrieved us from the roadside where we walked, and brought us to New York. She listened as her daughter told her about how the dentist insisted on paying for a hotel room, and for a phone call home. The phone call, my grandmother realized, was the answer to her prayer.

Instead of flying us back to Portland, my grandparents agreed to call Keith's family in New Hampshire. Keith's father, my grandfather's nephew, reluctantly agreed to drive to the hotel in New York to retrieve us. Although Keith was fishing in Alaska at the time, he soon became my mother's savior in her stories.

When Keith's father arrived in New York, he thought he had been duped. "She's got boys, not girls," he called home to tell his wife after observing us with our shaved heads.

We stayed with Keith's family in New Hampshire for a short while before my grandparents' sent us the money to fly back to Portland. I don't believe my mother had a choice but to fly us home. My father, for a brief while, was granted legal custody of his missing daughters. How it all fell apart for him was never shared.

In the only other letter my father saved from this time period, his social worker wrote, "I'm really happy to hear that the kids are back with you, even though things don't seem to be resolved yet." Later in the letter these words appear, "The investigators in San Diego have decided to drop the matter so nothing will be happening here."

It seems my father, who lost us again soon after he got us back, had given up the will to fight. I read his resignation in the social worker's words, "I sure feel badly for you that you're losing the support of family and friends. It sounds like you're beginning to doubt the steps you've taken and, for whatever its worth, I don't think you have anything to apologize for. We deal with a lot of custody disputes where kids are simply used as pawns between parents out to hurt each other, but I've never felt that your motivation was anything other than a sincere concern for your kids' well-being."

These two letters reveal a hazy, but definite trail of a father's love that I thought was never mine. Within a matter of weeks after they were written, I was living in a small white house in Portland with my mother, Tara and Keith. We were no longer hiding from my father, but I was learning to replace him.

I wish I had clear memories of my life with the Hare Krishnas and our journey back to Portland. Just as I wish I could remember my early life with my father before we left him. Instead my mind rolls out small pieces of a landscape. Green grass spilling into blue pools of water. A palace filling with gold. When I reach deep inside my body, though, there is a contraction of emotions. The troubled feeling of memories buried.

I remember the texture and hue of my Tulsi beads, which were eventually cut free of my neck, and then lost over time. In my memory, the beads were small and irregular in shape and in their brown hue. When I would rub them between my fingers they felt rough, like small dried peas. Tulsi for Tulsidas, the boy of Indian lore abandoned by his father who blamed his infant son for the childbirth death of his mother. Tulsidas, who later sought harmony in life as he worked to unite the worshippers of Rama and Krishna.

When I was three, my mother dressed me like the god Krishna for Halloween. In the photograph she took of me, I am wearing a wig of long black curls and my body is made blue, like the god's, with a turtleneck and tights. Around my waist I wear a dhoti of yellow cloth, wrapped like a skirt, with a light-blue sash. Strings of beads hang from my neck, arms and ankles. I look comically cute as the child-god before his face turned blue and beautiful.

Fragments

love
plays
In photographs
hiding
from the
camera
inside
smiles
a family of four in the division of
love

In the summer of 1976 Keith completed his contract work on a fishing boat in Alaska, and moved in with us. Although he was only twenty-three, Keith showed no signs of shying away from his new role as head of our household. In a photograph taken in September, Tara and I sit together between Keith's legs on the top step in front of our home in Portland. He is reading a picture book to us and smiling happily at my mother, who is taking the photograph. Tara and I, with our short, spiky hair, look like boys as we peer shyly without smiles at the camera.

When I recall our early years living, I recall mostly apprehension. Keith, who was taller than our father by about six inches, had a foreboding presence about him. His hands were large and strong; his voice deep and demanding of respect. If we smiled at him, Keith smiled back. If we ignored him, Keith grew sulky, or turned angry.

When Keith was happy, it was easier for us to be happy. On Saturdays, Keith, Tara and I would roll our red wagon out of the shed, and pull it behind us as we searched the roadsides for littered treasure. At the corner store at the end of the street, we'd lug our haul inside, and Tara and I would watch with anticipation as our bottles and cans were exchanged for coins. We never kept the money, but immediately traded it in for treats. Those were happy memories.

While living with him in Portland, Tara and I learned that Keith could be fun and charming, but he could also be careless and harsh. We had to tread softly around him, least we provoke anger in his voice. As people do, Keith made mistakes, and sometimes they caused others harm. One day, as we were leaving to go somewhere in his big green truck, Keith shut Tara's thumb in the truck door.

I remember climbing up first onto the long, slippery backseat, through the open door, waiting for Tara to join me. I watched as Tara, like me, pulled herself first onto the floor, and then, with her left hand on the doorframe, began to push her body up beside mine.

I saw Tara's hand linger a second too long as Keith strong arm swung the door shut in his eagerness to leave. Tara's cry beat my heart into alarm, and I watched as a tiny red river began to flow down her arm.

"It was me," my mother told Tara many years later in defense of Keith, "who shut your hand in the door." Tara and I, though, both remember the swing of his arm.

Months later, we left Oregon in the same green truck. It was the summer of 1978, and I was not yet five-years-old. My memory of the minutes before we drove away from our home, the state of my birth, and all of my relatives, takes the form of our white house as it looked from the side of the road, through the open window of the back seat of Keith's truck. In this scene, when I bring it forth, the front door is always open, revealing a hallway that extends into darkness; a brown shadow of emptiness that is mirrored in the shut windows.

It is the ball that changes. Sometimes, when I recall the moment when the truck begins to pull forward, and the house slowly moves away from us, I look through my window with my four-year-old eyes to see a large rubber ball, like the over-sized beach balls held inside big wire bins at grocery stores during summer-time. My ball is the color of the universe, deep purples swirled into indigo and dotted with a billion white stars. As we pull away in Keith's truck, I see my ball caught in the arms of the tree beside the home we are leaving behind. At other times, when this day comes back to me, the ball sits at rests after a roll, halfway down the hallway inside the house, caught in the shadow of emptiness. Always, though, it is just out of reach, and always when I see it in memory, I feel the tug inside to return; to go back and retrieve what we left behind.

The memory of the drive across the country from Oregon to New Hampshire is the feel of tires turning across three thousand miles of pavement. Before we left, my mother strung a make-shift curtain across the width of the cab, separating the front bench seat from the back, where my sister and I spent the long journey with books and pillows. The curtain, a soft piece of cotton cloth covered in cream and peach paisley swirls, was suspended on a thin rope and halved so that it could be pulled to the sides or left hanging while we slept.

Tara and I took turns sleeping on the floor, which we cushioned with blankets and pillows, creating a make-shift bed on the hard black surface upon which our breathing matched the steady hum of tires laboring over pavement as we fell into slumber. Naturally, we both preferred the vinyl of the seat with its slippery softness cushioning the bumps of the road beneath our bodies. From the seat we could look out the windows, or, if the curtain was parted, at the back of our mother's head. Sometimes our mother would sit in the middle of the front seat, close to Keith, who drove, her long brown hair hanging in waves down her back or pulled loosely into braids.

We arrived at the top of a small hill in Henniker a week after we left Portland, and set up home in the form of a tepee on the land Keith had purchased with his best friend, our new neighbor Jack, using money they had made while fishing together in Alaska. Our white canvas home looked like a traditional Native American tepee, although our floor was not the bare earth, but a wooden platform. In the center, supporting the canvas from the top, stood the stripped trunks of three narrow trees, around which the canvas was secured with rope. The tepee tipped to one edge of the wooden platform upon which it rested, and a long pole extended from the apex at an angle down to the ground. An attempt to stabilize the structure against collapse.

Inside the tepee there were no partitions for rooms, and from that summer and into the fall when the night air turned chill, we did our best to live together as a family of four in our conical room without windows. The door, a contraption made of screening framed with wood, along with the white of the canvas, allowed muted sunlight to filter in, creating an ambiance of a smoke filled room without the odor. Instead, the air inside held a musty, damp feel, like a tent the morning after it has been fully occupied. When it rained, the water would drip down the middle, through the cracks between the canvas and poles, and puddle into dark circles on the gray boards, and around the edges where we slept on straw mats.

Our kitchen and bathroom were both outside. An open-faced shed doubled as storage for firewood (to be used later in the small cabin Keith was building for our next home) and a kitchen. In front of the stacked cordwood there was a small refrigerator for our milk, eggs and tofu. We had electricity wired up to the shed, but no running water. Instead, our water was pumped by hand from a well dug by Keith, and my sister and I were bathed outside in a large metal wash-basin. Once or twice a week, the four of us drove to New England College to take showers.

Without plumbing, we lacked a conventional toilet. For the first several weeks, we relieved ourselves over a hole dug in the ground, then later, when Keith finished building it, we had an outhouse made of pine. We were living the hippie lifestyle my mother and Keith were embracing, including a meat-free diet and marijuana plants hidden in the woods. It was not unlike how we lived in Cave Junction with the father we had left behind. A not-so-distant life Tara and I were forbidden to talk about.

In Henniker, my mother and Keith grew their own yogurt cultures, and for breakfast we ate the soured cream with my mother's fresh granola and a drizzle of honey. We grew our own sprouts, in pots of earth perched near sunlight, and my mother baked bread, filled with a hearty mixture of grains, oats and sunflower seeds, in the woodshed oven.

We belonged to a food co-op, and each week the four of us would drive into town to collect thick squares of tofu in sheet-rock buckets of water, sacks of bulgur, white blocks of cheddar cheese and, for a special treat, single-serving cartons of blueberry and strawberry kefir. I loved the sweet bite of the kefir, and thought the stir-fried tofu-and-rice dinners, or "piles" as Keith called them, tolerable. What I couldn't stomach was the dish of cooked bulgur mixed with green peas my mother made all too often when I was a young child. The gooey mixture never failed to make my belly heave in protest with each bite I had to force down my throat. Keith, though, adhered to the strict rule that everything that was put on our plates must be consumed.

During the two years we lived in Henniker, I remember my sister and I getting head lice (my mother recalls this happing in Oregon, while we were in nursery school), as well an intestinal parasite that wreaked havoc on our digestion, and added to the horror of the already unpleasant routine of going to the bathroom outside. Perhaps in an attempt to rid our bodies of the worms, my mother administered enemas to me and Tara. Or, perhaps it was because of constipation, as the enemas persisted, as did my reluctance to go to the bathroom outside when the sun went down.

While Tara and I tried our best to transition back into the hippie lifestyle, remembering with longing our indoor toilet and TV at our last house in Portland, our mother and Keith made every effort to embrace their chosen lifestyle. Sometimes, they would even take photographs of us while we were going to the bathroom. To me, the photographs hint at something deeper and more troubling. They remind me of the feelings of the small child who was not understood by the photographer, and that perhaps her emotions were not even considered.

I have two pictures in the album my mother made for me that feature me going to the bathroom. In both, I appear, at first glance, to be smiling. The earlier photograph was taken when I was four-and-a-half. In the image, I squat on the porcelain rim of the toilet in the bathroom of our final home in Portland. My right hand holds the open door as though threatening to close it against the face of the voyeur, while my left hand grips the edge of the exposed bowl where my bare feet curl over the basin. I am naked, but over the photograph in the album my mother placed a sparkled sticker of a gold heart to hide my private parts.

The second photograph was taken three years later. Now seven, my hands grip the edge of the wooden seat of our outhouse. This time I am clothed. My red t-shirt and shorts, pulled down to just above my knees, reveal that it is summer. The sun from the window angles its light across my face and down my arms. As I look at this image of my younger self, I study a face brightened by the sun and try to find clues hidden in the dark pupils of my eyes. I follow the line of my smile and realize it is not real. Although my lips are open, they spread horizontally, their corners refusing to curl.

Sometimes I try to remember all of the bathrooms I experienced during the earliest years of my life, both indoors and out. They surface often in my dreams; taking on different forms, but always premised upon fear. In my slumber, I struggle to find a portal of privacy to relieve my aching body, a proper seat with a hole, and a handle to flush my waste. My body, it seems, cannot forget.

When bathrooms visit me in my dreams, I search for an elusive privacy, and a place to release the waste of accumulated fears and insecurities held inside of my body. Sometimes I dream of wooden benches without holes, or wander through labyrinthian buildings looking for a room with a toilet. When I find one, the walls disappear. Doors come down, and stalls are revealed, open and exposed. If I sit, the hole closes below me. Waste clogs receptacles. It soils my hands.

My first memory of going to the bathroom is over the dark hole in the ground in Henniker. I can recall crouching over this crude toilet at the age of four, and then five, trying not to breathe. Trying not to let my body fall in and never return. That is what I remember, the darkness underneath my naked bottom, the childhood fear of falling, and the stench of excrement. Later, after the hole was filled and we had an outhouse just like our neighbor Jack's, the fear of falling stayed with me.

In the outhouse, I was able to sit securely on a board, but still, when I dared to look down between my legs at the sawdust covered mounds upon the ground, I worried that if I wasn't careful my body would descend into the dark hole filled with flies and feces. Secretly, I prayed for the day to arrive when we would have a real bathroom like my friends had at their houses, but that day wouldn't come for a while.

When we moved into the small wooden cabin Keith built for us in Henniker, before the first snow fell in late fall, we continued to use an outhouse as our toilet. During the two years we lived in Henniker, our cabin-like home was never finished, and the "plumbing" remained outdoors. We urged water out of the earth with the labor of our arms, spilling it out of the metal mouth of the outdoor pump like regurgitated rain. A shower-head was eventually installed by Keith on the side of our home, and on warm days we would wash naked in the open-air with hot water heated by the sun.

The interior of this cabin-home appears to me in memory in the form of exposed wooden walls and beams, with muted light filtered through rows of paned windows. Keith's grandmother, my maternal grandfather's sister, visited us once while we were living in Henniker. After she left, she called her brother to tell him of her horror at our living conditions. "They're living in a shed barely bigger than a bathroom," she told my grandfather, "That's no way to raise children." My grandfather, the man I called "Poppy," became outraged with the news, but my mother would not hear it. "We're fine," she told them. "How we live is none of your business."

I started kindergarten, and my sister, first grade, while we were still living in the tepee. In kindergarten, I learned to count and write simple words, like the other children. On large pieces of manila paper I colored self-portraits, and drew pictures of my new family of four. There is no evidence in my drawings of the father I left behind in Oregon in my school-work. At home, Tara and I were forbidden to talk about our birth father. "It makes Keith feel sad," my mother would tell us. "Like you don't love him. He wants to be your father now." I can recall the frequent pout of Keith's mouth; the hurt expression of his blue eyes. I don't remember anyone ever asking what made me sad, though, or what made me hurt inside.

When I drew pictures in school, I allowed myself to enter the world of fantasy. I colored my body my favorite color red, and imagined I was a beautiful ballerina, or a gypsy with rainbow skirts. With crayons, and later, written stories, I created the world of my daydreams where I danced in pools of sunshine with fairies, played inside a rainbow treehouse, and ran away with my mother and sister to a magical land.

Occasionally, while we were living in Henniker, I experienced true happiness. One day, while we were still living in the tepee, Keith and my mother took Tara and me for a walk down the tree-shaded path through the woods to visit Jack and his girlfriend, Sandy, who was as my kindergarten teacher's aide. As we walked through the woods from our land to Jack's, I studied the ground, as I often did, for the circles of light where I knew fairies liked to dance. I concentrated on stepping without sound, while my eyes searched patches of tiny blue-white flowers that look like stars. This, I knew, was where the fairies hid. I felt their presence in the shadows of the blooms. I could almost see their tiny bodies camouflaged against the green stems. I imaged my fairies to be beautiful girls with blond curls and dresses made from petals. The wings of my fairies were clear and veined like the dragonflies my mother loved. Always, though, they stayed hidden, their shadows dancing and teasing me beneath the canopies of flowers.

As we neared the end of the path through the woods, I concentrated harder on finding the fairies so my eyes would not stray to the places where the hemlocks came together and made dark shadows. Somewhere to my left, in those shadows, was the old well Keith and Jack warned us never to go near. I worried about stumbling into that well almost as much as I worried about tipping back into the dark, smelly hole in the ground that was our toilet, so I never ventured off the path alone.

When we reached Jack's, we found him outside his own tepee, miniature-sized and positioned in front of his house. He wore a large grin on his face, and as we drew near, he opened the door flap of the tepee. I quickly forgot about the fairies now dancing shamelessly in the sunlight without me. Kittens filled the small conical room, curling into balls of white and brown, rolling like tumbleweed over each other, then hopping onto wooden boxes to swat their siblings as they ran past.

"You girls can choose two," Keith told us as he stood beside Jack and smiled through the open flap.

It was nearly impossible for me to make a decision. If I could have, I would have taken them all. Before it was time to leave, my sister and I settled on an all-white female and a male tabby with gold

31

and black stripes. As we walked back through the woods, I held the little white kitten tightly against my chest while my sister cradled her brother. There was no need to look for the fairies; my complete attention was devoted to my new charge.

While we walked home, the four of us took turns suggesting names for our first pets. I looked down at the squirming mound of white fur in my arms and thought of the flowers the fairies love. "How about Star," I said. My mother, in turn, suggested Hanuman for the tabby, after the monkey god who, as a child, tried to steal the sun.

I was thrilled with our new pets. Even when they grew into adult-sized cats, my sister and I would borrow dresses from our dolls and squeeze them over the heads of Star and Hanuman. Our pets would endure our loving tortures like troopers, running only when we released them, their tails sticking out like flags as they raced up the trees to freedom.

We only had Hanuman for about a year and a half. One day, he never came home, and his body was discovered a short time later behind a neighbor's house. Hanuman, my mother and Keith told us, had mistaken rat poison for a snack. I was quietly devastated by the loss of Hanuman and thought my neighbors should be punished for murdering my favorite pet. It didn't matter to me that the poison was intended for rodents. It only mattered that my beloved cat had been able to eat it. I mourned the loss of Hanuman with a fierce silence that lasted long after we buried him in our backyard. I still had Star, though, who went with us when we moved to Canterbury, where she too began to wander until she eventually never came home.

The girl who learned to be silent

listened closely to words
with the fierce loyalty of a daughter's love
catalogued narratives
behind
hesitation. And,
Many years later, birthed the
words waiting

In the early years of my life, I was raised on a healthy vegetarian diet supplemented by the indigestible stories told by my mother. After we moved three thousand miles away from my father and relatives, my mother began to share tales of abuse.

"I just had to get away from them all," she would periodically confess to me and Tara. "I don't want to raise you girls around them."

"Dave [my father] is a loser. He never cared about you girls and treated me like a doormat."

"My mother's crazy."

"I had a tough childhood. My father used to beat me and my brothers when he was angry."

"Mostly my brothers, but sometimes me," she would sometimes add. "One time, he was beating Dan so badly, I stepped in the way to stop him. I got so many bruises, I was afraid to change in the locker room for gym class."

"My mother can be really mean," my mother told me and Tara. "She used to call me stupid and dumb. She made me feel worthless. Just like Dave did when we lived together," she added in reference to our father. "He always used to put me down."

"He doesn't care about you two girls. He only cares about himself. I had to buy our clothes at secondhand stores, but he always had a closetful of new clothes and shoes."

"I can't even get him to pay child-support every month."

I listened to my mother's words in silence, beside my sister, who I knew could only be sharing my turmoil. Although it was somewhat easier to despise my father, as the memory of him hurting my mother lingered in my body and in my mind, my mother's stories about her parents filled me with confusion and guilt. Her words contradicted the few memories I had of them, which were filled with the unconditional and indulgent love of grandparents.

35

I never told my mother that her words caused confusion, sadness and a growing tumor of pain inside of me. I never told her they hurt me, and made me feel as though I too were being beaten. My mother, in turn, never asked if Tara and I minded the sharing of her stories, or showed any sign that she cared about the impact they might have on her young daughters. We were, from a young age, our mother's confidants. Instead of a therapist, or a best-friend to confide in, she had us. And what she shared with us in confidence, we were not allowed to share with others.

"Don't tell anyone that we're related," she'd tell me and Tara, referring to her relationship with Keith. "It's none of their business."

"Don't let anyone see the marijuana plants," our mother and Keith would remind us often. "If someone asks, tell them they're tomatoes."

I didn't want to tell anyone about my mother's stories of abuse. They hurt too much to share. As I listened to my mother's words, I tried to forget about what we had left behind in Oregon. I tried to believe, like she often told us, that we were lucky Keith had come into our lives.

"I don't know where we'd be without him," she'd often say.

Sometimes, though, I allowed myself to think about that possibility. About what life would be like if we were still living in Portland, in a house nearby my cousins and grandparents. It was another one of my daydreams I didn't talk about. Instead, I did my best to pretend we had a better life in New Hampshire than we would have if we had stayed in Oregon. And, I did my best to play the role of a respectful and loving daughter.

Tara and I were not children who had tantrums or rages, they were simply not permitted. The role of petulant child was reserved for Keith from the time he entered into our family. Keith's emotions could quickly surge with the force of a tsunami, and were in constant check by the three of us.

"He's sensitive," my mother would tell Tara and me if Keith was angry with us, "he feels badly when you don't treat call him dad and treat him like he's your father."

The explosions of rage occurred in the moments when we forgot our place. When Tara or I looked away when Keith was speaking to us, or when we failed to respond with conviction and respect. "I can't hear you," Keith would bellow. "Speak louder." "Look me in the eye when I'm talking to you."

When we overlooked him in favor or our mother, Keith would remind us, "I am your father now, you need to ask me."

If a rule was broken or forgotten, Keith used his hands. An errant elbow on the table during a meal often brought the swing of his hand to topple it. Lips turned in sass triggered the clench of his fingers around our throats.

As a young child, I learned to act with caution around Keith and to treat him like the revered ruler of the family he wanted to be. If Keith was unhappy, we were all unhappy. Tara and I rarely dared to speak of the father Keith had replaced, or of the family we still loved and missed back in Oregon. If we did, Keith would turn sullen and angry. In his mind there was no room for two fathers in our hearts.

Perhaps if we had been boys, it would have been different. Keith never tried to hide the fact that he would have preferred to have two boys instead of two girls. In fact, he often joked about his disappointment with other adults. "I would have liked to have raised boys," he would chuckle, "but I seemed to have inherited two girls."

One day, Keith brought home yellow Tonka trucks for me and Tara. They were used, but still shiny and nearly new. Twin dump trucks, meant for barreling over earth with their thick black tires.

"You can play with them in the sand pile," he told us, and for a few days we tried our best to pretend we loved his gifts. Tara and I filling the backs of our trucks with sand, then dumping them into neat piles before we began the process of filling and dumping all over again. It got old faster than Keith wanted it too, and it was hard for him to hide his disappointment when we favored playing with our dolls, stuffed animals, and the cats.

Keith, though, never gave up trying to mold us into the two boys he wished we were. Frequently, when he had work to do on a building project, and Tara and I were not in school, Keith would ask us to accompany him to his workshop. "Why don't you girls come with me," he would tell us, "I'll show you how to use a jigsaw." We dared not say we'd rather not. Instead, Tara and I allowed Keith to guide our reluctant and nervous fingers as we cut boards into shapes, sawdust flying past our goggles and into our nostrils.

"I hate going to the workshop," Tara and I would whisper to each other, but never in the presence of Keith or our mother, who often reminded us, "He feels like you don't love him enough."

When I think of the five-year-old girl struggling to love the man who wanted me to call him dad, I remember the time Keith took me for a walk in the woods beside our tepee.

It's cold under the trees where there is no sunlight. Beside me is the man who says he is my father, but to me he is like a bear. When he moves, my heart jumps into my throat. It is a bird, and if I open my mouth it will fly away.

I want to rub my palms against the bumps on my arms and legs so they will disappear and I can feel warm again, but I am afraid to do anything but walk. I don't like being alone with Keith. I wish my mother and sister had come with us, but Keith wouldn't let them. He said he wants to talk only to me. So I try to focus on the brown patchwork of the forest floor. My feet crunch the old leaves while I search for the roots of trees in the dirt, and try not to trip.

"Alethea," Keith's voice electrifies my body and I start to shake. He has stopped walking. "Can you look at me for a minute?"

I don't like looking into Keith's face when he is upset with me, and the boom in his voice makes my heart leap and hide. I lift my head and try to look into his eyes. Keith's face is full of shadows and his mouth isn't smiling. Already I know I have done something wrong.

"You know I love your mother, don't you?" I nod my head and study the dirt in front of my feet. I've never doubted Keith's love for my mother.

"Alethea, please look at me while I'm talking to you." My head feels heavy like a rock, but I turn my face again to peer into the deep blue eyes that he often tells me are just like my own.

"You know I care about you and your sister, and I'm trying real hard to be your father. You know, Alethea, this isn't easy for me."

Inside my head I try to imagine what it would be like to be Keith and move into a family that is not really yours, but instead I feel the force of water building behind the walls of my eyes. I don't know if I have enough love to give him so that he can be happy with me. I don't know if I have enough love inside of me to make us all into a real family of four.

"I don't think you're doing enough to make this work, though. I'd like you to try harder? Can you promise me you'll do that?"

"Okay," I whisper toward the earth below me.

"Alethea, I'm up here." I feel the strength of Keith's hand under my chin, lifting it to the sky. "Are you willing to work at this with me?"

"Yes," I make my voice louder, hoping Keith can't hear the shake of my body, hoping it's enough to turn us around so we can go back to my mom and my sister.

As we walk back through the trees, Keith starts to whistle and I know he is happy again, but my heart is still flying into the walls of my body. I wish I knew how to settle it down. I wish I knew how to make us into a happy family. I only know that I am not doing enough.

Proof

the photos
collect two skinny girls grinning
in red-and-blue bathing suits, the
weight of water

celebrates

my life
compared to girls
in pink dresses and
lily-white socks folded in lace

My mother, Tara and I returned to Oregon for a week in the summer of 1979. We stayed with my maternal grandparents, who paid for our airfare. A year had passed since we moved to New Hampshire, and in those twelve months I had learned to call Keith "dad." I had also learned not to talk about the father who still phoned us every few weeks to check-in, unless it was to speak of him, like my mother did, in unfavorable terms.

I decided, as I flew through the white cushions of clouds on an airplane for the first time, that I didn't want to see my father in Oregon. Instead, I daydreamed about playing with my cousins, and swimming in the cool, chlorinated water of my grandparents' pool.

When we landed at the airport in Portland, a party of relatives had gathered to greet us. My grandparents were there, along with a handful of aunts and uncles, a couple of cousins, and my father. I watched my mother greet her relatives with restrained embraces and smiles, and decided she must love them at least a little bit. My father, she pretended not to see, even though he came over to hug me and Tara.

Spending time with my father and his side of my family during this trip takes the form of a vague, nearly absent memory. My cousin Linda appears in a photograph swimming in my grandparents' pool. Proof that she had come over with my father to visit for at least an afternoon. In a separate photograph from my father's collection, my sister and I grin shyly at the camera. Two skinny little girls in red-and-blue bathing suits, which sag like loose skin with the weight of water.

That week back in Oregon is now a blur of swimming with cousins, watching cartoons in the basement den with Poppy, and the scene of a family reunion with my mother's relatives. Tara and I in our second-hand clothes appear in photos standing next to our boy first and second cousins, and our cousin Cindy in her perfectly new clothes of frilly pink flowers and white lace. Our hair now long and blond matches the hue of our cousins and second cousins, and we almost look like we belong.

The Sunday of our visit, though, plays back to me in a vivid narrative. That day, my grandparents decided to take Tara and me to church. My grandparents, devout Catholics, rarely, if ever, missed a Sunday service, but Tara and I had never, before that day, been to church. We were not even baptized, much to my grandmother's dismay, as my mother became an atheist before she left her family home. Where my mother was on that day, I do not know.

Before we left for church, I followed my grandmother into her bedroom and watched while she stood before her dresser mirror clipping yellow-and-white daisies on her earlobes to match the flowers on her polyester suit. I wanted to clip metal flowers on my pierced ears, but I was too shy to ask. Instead, I sat quietly on the edge of my grandparents' bed and peered into the depth of the mirror. Behind my grandmother's reflection, I could see the gold figure of Christ stretched upon a metal cross, his head bowed in exhaustion toward Earth.

I knew little of this man who hung on the wall above my grandparents' bed and watched them sleep, but I knew my grandmother knelt down on the dark green carpet of her floor and prayed to him before she went to bed, and while she prayed she asked him to watch over and protect me and my sister. I knew she thought we should do the same, as she sometimes told us, with a shake of her head, that we were growing up in a household without God.

I wore a dress for the occasion, with brown buckled shoes over my mostly white tights, wishing that I had shiny black shoes and lace socks like my cousin Cindy. As we slid across the green vinyl of my grandmother's car, she turned around to look at us. "Now remember," she said, "you girls need to be real quiet at church. I want you to sit nicely with me and Poppy. No talking or fooling around."

I am sure we obeyed, rarely did we disobey, but it felt like an eternity sitting sandwiched between our grandparents, while we tried to understand the words of the priest and the songs that were sung by everyone around us. I knew Tara and I were in a place where we did not belong.

Because we were not baptized, my sister and I were not offered the body of Christ, or the red wine of his blood. Instead, at the end of the service we stood beside our grandparents and waited for the turn we never got, watching as each person before us opened a mouth to the bone-colored wafer placed by the priest upon their waiting tongues.

When my grandmother's turn arrived I studied her, trying to memorize her motions. I quickly forgot the order of her hands across her chest after she closed her lips, but it didn't matter.

After my grandmother turned from the priest, she whispered in my ear, "Close your mouth, Alethea. You can't have one," and hurried me back down the aisle.

***

At the end of that summer, after we returned home from Oregon, I celebrated my sixth birthday with my two best friends, Tina and Jenny. Tina was moving up to first grade in the fall, but Jenny and I were going to be in Readiness together. Readiness was a program, popular in Henniker during the 1970s, for children considered "not yet ready" for the academic or emotional demands of first grade. I was in the latter category, but I never quite shook my self-imposed stigma that I somehow wasn't smart, or good enough.

At the age of six, I was becoming aware of how different my life was compared to the lives of the other little girls I knew. Back in New Hampshire, I thought often of my cousin Cindy in her pretty pink dresses and pants, and those lily-white socks that folded in a row of lace around her shiny black shoes. I envied the perfect life I was sure my cousin lived. A life filled with fancy store bought clothes, beauty pageants, modeling, and dance classes, orchestrated by two doting parents who tended to their daughter inside a two-storied house with painted walls, carpeted stairs, and indoor bathrooms.

Most of my wardrobe consisted of second-hand clothes. When we wore them out, or out-grew them, my mother would drive me and Tara to the Salvation Army store in Concord. While my mother sorted through the racks of little girl clothing, I rummaged through the bins of baby dresses for my dolls. I grew to dread these shopping trips when I began to worry about the possibility of one of my friends driving by and seeing us in the parking lot. At the Salvation Army store my mother could buy clothes by the bagful, but the clothes never shined new and pretty like my cousin Cindy's, or my friend Tina's.

When I would go to Tina's house, I would absorb myself in her coveted life. Tina lived in a large white home in the middle of a big yard full of mown grass and flower gardens. Tina had her own bedroom attached to a closet filled with pretty clothes that came new from department stores, and in her living room sat a color TV. When I would visit Tina, her mother would sometimes let us stay inside and watch cartoons, even when the sun shone full with warmth.

It was Jenny, though, who gave me the Barbie doll on my birthday. When I opened the wrapper to reveal the slim, blond woman modeled miniature-sized in flesh-colored plastic, I glanced nervously at my mother, who frowned.

After Tina and Jenny finished pushing pieces of brown carob cake around their plates, we took the doll outside to the stream beside my home. On the package, Barbie, who wore only a bright pink one-piece bathing suit, was shown swimming in a pool, so the three of us took turns floating her where the water collected into a tiny pond.

After my friends left, my mother lifted Barbie from her place of rest on the couch, "I'm sorry Alethea, I can't let you keep this."

"Why?" I asked, as my heart sank inside my chest. Even though my mother had told me before how she felt about Barbies and dolls with breasts, I hoped I might be able to keep this one.

"Because I don't want you playing with Barbie dolls. They're not appropriate for little girls."

"But she's a gift," I said even though I knew I was fighting a losing battle. "All of my friends are allowed to have Barbies," I added quietly.

"I don't care what your friends play with. I don't want *you* to play with them." The discussion, I knew, was over.

I never found out what happened to Barbie, but I sometimes imagined her lying naked and cold in the trash under cartons of kefir. I wasn't a child who received a lot of gifts, and this was not one I wanted to lose.

A few days after my birthday, I started Readiness. There had been ten kids in my morning kindergarten class, and there were twelve children in my Readiness class. Approximately half of the students from the two kindergarten classes did not advance to first grade that year, but growing up, I felt like I was the only one.

47

Memories of Readiness come to me in the form of faded scenes from the playground and classroom, which was on the first floor of the elementary school, to the right of the entrance. When we would arrive, we would place our bags and shoes in the wooden cubbies along the wall. The playground had a painted hopscotch and one of those hand-pushed metal merry-go-rounds that are no longer considered safe for children. During recess my classmates and I would play "boys chase girls," a game I loved because the boys always wanted to chase me. That's what I remember, aside from the day one of the boys in my classroom wet his pants, the stain of urine spreading like a halo around his bottom as we sat in a circle on the gray rug.

After my year of Readiness was over, we left Henniker behind and moved to the small town of Canterbury, New Hampshire, exactly a mile down the road from where Keith grew up, and where his parents still lived. I never learned the specific reasons why we left Henniker, but I know Keith wanted to move back to his home town. He was also no longer best-friends with Jack. By the time we left Henniker, we were no longer walking the path to Jack's house to visit, and the only time Keith spoke about his former best-friend was in a voice filled with anger. Jack had done something to upset Keith, but when I, years later asked my mother what it was, she replied in vague terms about a disagreement over money. Jack, she added, had never been good with money. But, I wanted to remind her, neither had Keith.

I have always wondered if the day my mother, Jack, Tara and I spent at a pond without Keith and Sandy had something to do with the abrupt end of Keith and Jack's friendship. In my mind I can still see my mother swimming and laughing with Jack, like they were two children learning to play at love. By the time we left Henniker,

Jack was no longer dating Sandy, and we were no longer walking the path to the house next door.

The last time we visited Jack's house was by car, and it was not a happy occasion. I remember Jack standing outside on the grass as though waiting for our arrival. Inside our small VW Bug the silent air felt claustrophobic. When Keith pulled onto the lawn he told us to stay inside. With his eyes focused on Jack, he jumped out of the car and slammed the door shut with a backward swing of his arm. I watched with my breath held tight, Keith approach his former friend.

To me Keith looked like a grizzly bear defending his territory. Although I could not see his face, or make out his words from within the closed doors, I knew Keith was angry. He was too close to Jack, and his arms moved out from his sides, expanding his girth. When his voice broke through the metal and glass, I could feel its power. It was thunder, and I waited with my breath held tight, for the flash of light.

That's when the car began to roll, slowly down the slope of Jack's lawn. Jack, who was facing it, saw it first and turned away from Keith, rushing forward to stop it. Before his foot could reach the pedal to break the momentum, Keith overtook Jack, reaching in with one arm and pulling his former friend out as though he was the one who had put us in danger.

Without a word, Keith left Jack standing and looking stunned on his lawn, while he got in the driver's seat, slammed the door of the car, turned us around, and drove away. As we moved down the driveway, I peeked out the back window to see if Jack was okay. He had not moved from his place on the grass, and was watching us with a face filled with confusion and hurt. In that moment my heart brimmed with empathy for this man who, it seemed to me, had only tried to save us. Jack, in my memories, had always been kind and gentle, and I would miss his presence in our lives.

Remarried

home
too small to hold

me
I yearn to slip inside space
my arms
rock weight

When the four of us left Henniker to move to Canterbury, we again had only a plot of land. Our property was purchased from the parents of a girl named Margot, who would soon become my best-friend. Instead of putting up a te-pee while Keith built our new home, we moved in with his parents.

Our roles were quickly assigned in this new clan we had been brought into. While staying with Keith's parents, Tara and I were expected to do our part to earn our keep. We set the table before meals, and while we ate, Tara and I received instruction in the proper etiquette of table manners.

"No elbows on the table," Keith or his parents would remind us.

"Put your napkin on your lap, please."

"Don't chew with your mouth open, girls."

"Ask politely if you would like the ketchup, don't reach."

After everyone was finished eating, Tara and I would gather the plates, load the dishwasher and wash dishes. When it was time to vacuum or do laundry, we helped with these chores as well. Just as we did when we had our own home.

Sometimes Tara and I were sent to the town store, which was just a short walk up a hill from the house, to buy milk, eggs, bread, dried pasta, or whatever item was needed in the kitchen. I remember enjoying these errands, especially when Mr. Parker was working behind the counter. Mr. Parker owned the Canterbury Country Store, and when Tara and I would pay for our purchases he would reach under the counter into the glass jars of penny candy and slide two pieces across with our change. It was small gesture that never failed to make me feel special.

By the time our own house was finished enough for us to occupy it, we were eager to move in. Keith's father, in particular, seemed to have a difficult time welcoming us into his home. When he spoke, it was usually to his son or his wife. My mother, when we were alone with her, would remark about how much she knew Keith's father didn't want us there. Although I could tell Keith's mother was trying her best to adopt the role of grandmother to us, I could also tell his father would rather not be our grandfather. Never did he show us the unconditional indulgence of a grandparent's love, and in the rare moments when he did embrace us, I could feel repulsion.

Keith's father, I learned through stories shared from my mother and grandmother, harbored a grudge against his uncle, the grandfather I called Poppy. When they were boys, the two had lived in the same house like brothers for several years. According to Keith's father, Poppy was not very kind to him and would sometimes beat him up. I saw this resentment mirrored on the face he displayed toward my mother, Tara and me. His smile always appeared wider when saying goodbye to us, than when saying hello, and unlike Poppy, he was often gruff and grumpy in our presence.

A year later, when my mother married Keith, I would witness the family tension first-hand. The wedding took place on a sunny day in early June. The ceremony was held inside the small combination living room, dining room and kitchen of our unfinished home. Tara and I were assigned the roles of "strawberry girls" for the occasion.

The dress my mother sewed for me was a simple pink cotton frock, tucked in at the waist and at the end of the short sleeves where a row of white eyelet ruffles trimmed their ends. Above the eyelet, on the bottom of my dress, my mother stenciled a row of strawberries, connected by curves of green vines. Tara's dress, also made by our mother, was of white cotton patterned in a manufactured mix of berries on vines. Strawberry stencils rimmed her white vest.

Tara and I wore our dresses bare over tanned legs, our feet covered in white cotton fold-down socks (without lace) inside our black Morris-dancing shoes. Before the ceremony, my mother filled two small brown baskets with strawberry plants unearthed from her garden beside our outhouse, and planted them carefully with watered dirt. On the handles, she tied bows with thin strips of white and pink ribbons. When we lifted our baskets, we held them tight with both hands, their contents heavy from the life packed inside.

Instead of a wedding dress, my mother wore an ivory tank-top she crocheted, under a loose, sleeveless blouse made of the same linen as her home-made skirt. Her feet were also bare inside shoes that matched her daughters'. Keith, who was now officially my stepfather, shaved his beard for the event, leaving only his mustache and rows of bristles that descended in thick, scruffy lines down the sides of his cheeks. Above his new brown work-pants, he wore a shirt made by my mother, ivory cotton, opened wide at the neck.

Even though I knew very little about religion at the age of seven, I knew weddings were supposed to take place in churches, with lots of guests wearing fancy clothes. I thought my mother looked beautiful on her wedding day (to me she always looked beautiful), but I wanted to see her in a long white dress with a veil of lace covering her lovely face. I thought my stepfather, in turn, should be wearing a dark suit instead of new brown work pants. Although I sort-of liked the idea of being a strawberry-girl, I really wanted to be wearing a frilly white dress and lacy socks. I wanted shiny black shoes that buckled over a small heel, and I wanted to be holding a basket filled with pink rose petals instead of brown dirt and vines.

My sister and I were the only children I knew who were strawberry-girls, and we were the only girls I knew of who had attended their parents' wedding. A concept that, even at seven, I found more startling than exiting. At the time, I had only one friend with divorced parents and she lived with her brother and her mother, who had not yet remarried. I was the only child in my class with two fathers, a distinction that added to my feeling of being conspicuously different from my peers.

As I stood on the bumpy brick of the floor of our home with my strawberry plant cradled under my hands, the room felt tight and small. It felt too small to hold the dozen or so people gathered for the ceremony. My mother's parents and her youngest brother were the only family who had flown three thousand miles east for the event. Inside our small home, there was not enough space for the two related families who grouped separately like cliques of teenagers.

As I stood shyly beside my mother and new father, I wanted to be happy like my mother, whose face in my memory glowed like the sun. Instead, as I watched her slide a white gold band etched with two strands of wheat onto Keith's finger, then kiss him long on the lips, I yearned to slip inside the thin strip of space between them and wrap my arms tightly around her legs. To claim her, once again, as my own.

Secrets

always break free

peer out open windows
follow us

When we are alone, whispering

We are
real

Two weeks after the wedding, my father flew east to visit me and Tara. Of this visit, I can only remember two days. A drive to the seacoast, and a day spent at Benson's Wild Animal Park. Benson's, although much smaller in size, reminded me of the Portland, Oregon Zoo. Of all the animals we saw that day, my memory holds onto the giant tortoises, who I watched in fascination amble on thick legs in slow motion around their pen. I can recall my urge to climb on their hard bumpy backs and let them rock my weight slowly across Earth. This, according to the sign nailed to their fenced enclosure, was not allowed. Instead I ran the palms of my hands along the surfaces of their built-in homes, while I tried to guess how many years each one had lived.

Like the trips we would later make to the Portland Zoo during our annual summer visits to Oregon, our father allowed Tara and me to select one souvenir each from the gift shop at Benson's. We chose the same stuffed green turtles with shells quilted in flowers. It was, in my memory, a happy day.

Later in the week, my father took us to Hampton Beach. During the hour-and-a-half drive to the seacoast, I listened quietly while our father joked about how small the eighteen miles of New Hampshire coastline is compared to Oregon's three hundred. There was no disputing this fact, but while he talked, I felt my face redden in defense of the state I now called home.

When we arrived at Hampton, the wide sandy beach was, as always on a warm summer day, packed tight with swim-suited bodies. I can recall standing on the hot, white sand, and looking through the sea of bodies for a place to spread our towels. As we began to navigate our way to an open spot, Tara disappeared. Or maybe it happened later, but in my mind I recall this moment as the point of my alarm. Standing there with my father, I realized Tara was no longer with us. A surge of panic rose within me as I pulled on my father's arm to tell him she was gone.

In my memory, my father responded to the news of my sister's absence in slow-motion, like the giant tortoises at Benson's. His gaze wore a look of confusion, instead of the alarm I wanted, as he studied my face in his attempt to comprehend my words.

When finally he turned his head to take in the masses of people, he mumbled, "Are you sure?" There was a chasm of silence. "Maybe she just went for a swim."

"But she's supposed to be with us. She shouldn't be by herself," my small voice insistent in its plea for understanding.

I stopped searching through the crowds on the sand, and looked to the water. In my memory I am the one who first spotted Tara. I found her where the ocean rushes to meet the dry sand, swinging like a hammock over the waves. I recognized her thin, muscular form in its purple flowered bathing suit, which matched the one clung to my body. I watched, with my breath stilled and my feet stuck fast to the sand, my sister held beneath her arm pits, and by her ankles, as two young men laughed and swung Tara's body in tandem over the crashing waves. My sister, turned toward us, wore the face of terror. Like that day when I was two, sitting on Grammie's couch with my sister and cousin, I experienced the incapacitating impulse to save.

I knew I couldn't run down to the shore by myself to rescue Tara, so I tugged at my father's arm, and pointed once again to the waves and his daughter. Hoping, as I did, that he'd see the same cause for alarm.

Again, his response was too slow. "Are you sure she doesn't know them?" he asked.

The young men released my sister as we approached, and we never spoke of this terrifying event again, until many years later when I mentioned it to Tara. "I don't remember that day at all," she told me. Could such a vivid memory, I wondered, have been a dream, or had she simply blocked it out like so much of our childhood?

***

At the end of that summer, during Labor Day weekend, my mother, stepfather, Tara and I packed into our gold Honda Civic for our second annual trip to the "Island." Each summer until I was fourteen, and then once more when I was seventeen, my family drove three hours north into Maine to spend the long weekend on a one-acre private island. The island belonged to friends of my step-grandparents, and here we gathered annually with Keith's parents and his four brothers and their families on this small circle of land for three days.

The weekend began without incident. Before we left our house, my sister and I buckled into the backseat of our gold hatchback and quickly established the invisible line in the center, separating the two spaces we could each occupy. Next we broke out the package of powdered donuts, a rare treat, and dusted our faces with white sugar as we began the long drive. The radio, as it always was, was tuned to NHPR, until it disappeared somewhere near Maine, along with the donuts, and Tara and I began crossing the invisible line.

When we arrived at the campground near the lake, my sister and I entered the main building, a log cabin combination store and office, with our stepfather, to borrow the horn to signal our pick-up to the island from the mainland. Later, as we passed the lines of trailers, dragging our bags onto the dock in preparation, Tara and I whispered loudly in superior tones about how much luckier we were than the kids on the mainland who had to sleep in campers and share the beach with a bunch of people they didn't know. Secretly, I envied the merry laughter of those crowded campers, who happily pitched balls over nets and raced to the wooden raft that floated in the water.

It was nice to feel special, though, and I loved the blast of the horn, which turned the eyes of strangers in our direction when my stepfather walked to the end of the dock and squeezed its rubber bladder. Shyly, I scanned the beach to see who had heard, then peered the half-mile across the water to watch as my step-grandfather readied the sailboat to retrieve us. My eyes fixed on the end of the dock, which jutted out from the island like a long, brown tongue. Soon, across the still water, the faint roar of the motor could be heard.

When night fell on the island, my family packed into our green, "four-person" tent, and tried to slumber squished together in sleeping bags. With my stepfather and sister close by, and the bumpy ground beneath my body, sleep was elusive, and I covered my ears with my pillow in an attempt to block out their competing snores, which filled the nylon space. In the morning, we woke early with the sun, the air inside our tent wet and dense, as though we were encased in a damp towel, like mornings in the tepee back in Henniker.

We gathered with Keith's family around the stone fire-pit for breakfast, waiting with rumbling stomachs as my step-grandmother filled a cast iron pan with bacon and cooked it over the open flames until the meat shriveled into crispy curls. After carefully removing the bacon with metal tongs onto a plate, she scrambled at least a dozen eggs in the grease left inside. Even though we were still vegetarians, my family ate the eggs (delicious!) saturated in bacon fat, and passed over the sizzling ribbons of meat. On the small benches made from logs surrounding the fire pit, I sat beside my mother and Tara while we ate and watched the flames jump between the burning logs.

After breakfast, Tara and I explored the island. It was cool and dark under the thick canopy of pine needles that did their best to block out the sun, and we tripped and skipped over roots as we covered its surface. When we reached the sandy cove, about ninety degrees from the dock, we claimed it as our own. Here we stripped free of our sweatshirts and long pants and buried our toes into the wet sand beside the shore. When our tender skin met the rough edges of freshwater mussels, we dug them free, watching as they closed their mouths in protest to being so rudely brought to the surface, away from the safety of their home of sand. Even though we could hear the laughter of the women, who sat sunning themselves on the dock with their wine coolers and bowls of chips, Tara and I would pretend we were alone on our island, perched on the backs of the big rocks inside the cove like pirates as we peered across the water at the tiny people moving along the shore.

After dinner on Sunday, our last night on the island, everyone gathered beside the fire and waited for my step-grandmother to bring forth the birthday dessert. Inside the aluminum pan was her signature cake, which she carried toward me as I sat beside my step-father's second youngest brother. The cake was made the same way for each relative's birthday, a layered concoction that began with crushed graham crackers mixed into a paste with butter, overlaid with a half-inch of whipped cream cheese mixed with more butter, and topped with freshly whipped cream and fruit. My stepfather's favorite dessert.

The cake that summer was halved by candles. Ten for me (an extra for good luck) and twenty-four for my step-uncle, whose birthday was also in August. I was fond of my stepfather's second youngest brother, who became our neighbor in Canterbury. Always he showed me a kind face with a smile that made his eyes shine like water in sunlight. That night, as he always did, he let me blow out most of the candles, even those that were not mine, then winked at me and gave me a pinch on my behind (again for good luck). While I shyly opened each gift that had been brought from New Hampshire I made sure, as my stepfather's eyes watched me closely, to thank each of my new relatives for their kindness.

Later that evening, after Tara and I brushed our teeth in the water at the edge of the island, then used the outhouse, we made our way to our tent. The sun had not yet set, and the men were still playing horseshoes in the middle of the island. As we passed near the pit, the sweet smoke of marijuana lifted through laughter and the sharp ring of iron hitting iron. I thought of the plants by our outhouse back home and the women's warning, "Don't go near the pit while they're playing horseshoes. It's dangerous."

We woke Monday morning tired and ready to return home to our own beds. After breakfast we packed bags and folded tents. Then, one family at a time, we loaded into the sailboat and motored to shore.

The ride home stretched out in long, slow miles. Tara and I, in our struggle for space, crossed the invisible line separating our two seats at least fifty times during the three hour drive. When we finally arrived at our house, I ran from the car, calling for Star, and our cat Tulsi, who had replaced Hanuman after we moved to Canterbury. The cats were nowhere to be found.

I am not sure who entered the door to our house first. It could have been any one of us, as our door was never locked. Perhaps that day we all went in together, each carrying a bag from our weekend away. When I stepped through our small foyer and into the main room downstairs, I knew something was wrong. My eyes took in the desk beside the couch, with its wooden drawers pulled, then traveled to the opened door of our refrigerator, revealing bare metal ribs. As I stood, surveying the aspects of the scene that did not belong, I felt fear take hold of my legs. I wanted to run and hide outside. Instead, I stood rooted to the hard brick, while my eyes tried to comprehend a pile of sand on the floor in front of our empty refrigerator.

When I realized my parents were moving throughout the house, cataloging its missing contents, my mind released my feet and followed them. The thirty-five millimeter camera normally stored in the desk downstairs was gone, as well as my stepfather's wedding ring, which he never wore, but kept tucked away in a small box on a shelf behind the hinged bookcase built into the wall at the top of the stairs.

I followed my parents' voices to their bedroom, running past the room I shared with my sister, to find them. Here I saw more empty drawers, this time in the form of tiny wooden rectangles, pulled free from my mother's jewelry box. Hanging from the ceiling above their bed was the open square door to our unfinished attic space, and below it, on the quilt, spat out like unwanted dinner, was a pile of green plants that had been dried and picked from the buckets by the stream. Inside the still air, I could smell the sweet scent of sin. My heart made a leap into my throat as I realized someone now knew one of our big secrets.

The four of us went next to the bedroom I shared with Tara. When I stepped across the threshold, the first thing I noticed was the opened door of the closet. On the floor in front, knocked down from their places on the shelf, were the two denim wallets my mother had made for me and Tara. Even before I looked inside, I knew they were empty. Their zippers were unzipped, their sides flat against the floorboards. Every cent I had, aside from the pennies tucked safe inside the belly of my clay pig on my bookshelf, had been stolen, including the "rare" coins I had started to collect.

It was the dolls, though, that made me crumble. The wood of the shelf above my desk was naked and exposed where, before we left, six-inch department store dolls had sat side-by-side wearing dresses of Holland, Spain, Germany, Ireland and France. After that August afternoon, I never made another trip to Rich's department store with five dollars from my earned allowance and birthday money to purchase a tiny plastic girl from a foreign country. Instead, I sometimes imagined the little girl who must be playing with my dolls, after they were taken from me and given to her. I wondered if she too loved Spain the most, with her scarlet dress edged in black lace.

The loss of my dolls, my most prized possessions, was too much for me to bear. I ran out of my room, down the staircase and through the front door of the house. I didn't stop until my knees folded into the brown dirt of the driveway, where I let my grief break away in sharp, hard tears.

When a police officer arrived to file a report of our missing possessions, I was called inside to sit at the table with the rest of my family. The list was short. My parents mentioned the camera and my mother's jewelry. Tara, the seven dollars plus change, including the approximate number of "rare" coins taken from our two wallets. I, in turn, quietly named each of my missing dolls. After, I followed my parents, who led the officer through the rooms of our small house. As we ascended the stairs I thought about the dried plants that were not supposed to be on my parents' bed, holding my breath inside my chest until I dared to peek into the room. I exhaled relief when I saw the marijuana had disappeared from the quilt. The once open mouth of the attic, now shut tight against the ceiling.

When I was an adult, and asked her about the robbery, mother told me that she and my stepfather had a suspicion of who had robbed us, but wouldn't share the person with me. She also told me that my memory of the dried marijuana plants on their bed was not real. "Dad didn't grow pot for very long," she said. "And it was only for his own use. He never sold it." Her own body, she added, could not tolerate the drug.

My mother's words contradict my memories and those of my sister. Tara remembers driving to a neighboring town with our step-father to drop off a dried bundle of sweet-smelling leaves, and I have never forgotten the black car that didn't belong at the end of our driveway. I remember watching this strange car from the field in front of our house as a young child, with its open trunk like a mouth waiting to be filled.

"That car was there to pick up one of our kittens," my mother told me when I tried to press my point.

I found my mother's explanation, sent through the safe distance of email, desperate. It was, for me, not worth the frustration of telling her that I knew she was lying; that our only cat to have kittens was Daphne, who had her litter when I was seventeen, long after the plants beside the stream were gone. I didn't want to listen to my mother struggle in an attempt to explain why a trunk would be open for a kitten. She had already shown me that her secrets were more important than my truths.

Question

People

who agree

to pretend
feel the heat of their pupils
piercing skin. whisper

"Why?" test
a pause

They probably are haunted
in the night

ghosts
constructs of the mind that
doubt words
travel the road to
Truth

Margot and I became best friends after we discovered we were going to be neighbors. On that early summer day, as Margo stood on the dirt beside the foundation of my soon-to-be home, she positioned herself as leader. I liked her instantly. Margot reminded me of Sarah, my first friend in Henniker, with her dimpled smile, curly hair, and lashes that framed eyes the color of chocolate. Margot had everything a little girl could want. She lived in a large house with her own bedroom, where she slept like a princess in a canopied bed. Attached to her bedroom was her very own bathroom with a fluffy pink rug that hugged the legs of her toilet and sink. In her yard, Margot had a treehouse I coveted, tucked into the arms of an oak. Nearby, in a fenced enclosure, grazed her very own pony. Margot was living the life I wanted, or so I thought.

In the arms of the oak, tucked inside her treehouse, Margot told me her first secret. After we climbed the ladder, on that fateful day, we peered out the open windows, and down the hole to check for spies. It would not do to have someone we knew walking along the roadside, or worse, one of Margot's siblings spying on us from the grass beneath.

When we were certain we were alone, Margot whispered through the empty air, "Guess what?"

"What?" Already my heart had begun to pound its excited fist against my t-shirt.

"I have a cousin who is a *real* princess," Margot paused for effect before she added "her name is Sarah."

My new best friend looked me full in the face, her eyes sparkling as she dared me to doubt her words, which of course I didn't.

The idea of someone I knew having a cousin who was a princess seemed slightly improbable, yet wildly romantic to my seven-year-old imagination. I really wanted to believe Margot, so I gave her the benefit of doubt. Perhaps Margot really was the luckiest girl in the world. I loved the idea of her cousin, who shared the name as my first best friend, being a real princess. Even if it made me envy Margot more than I already did.

"You do?" I asked. "She is?! Can I meet her? Does she live in a castle?"

Margot laughed with the air of superiority, "Of course you can't! She lives in England."

I knew England only as a mysterious and ancient land of castles and knights. A place that seemed quite likely to be filled with kings, queens, princes and princesses, one of whom might, just might, be related to my wonderful new friend, Margot.

Before we climbed down the ladder Margot made me swear that I wouldn't tell anyone about her princess cousin. If I did, she whispered, something bad might happen to her family. I knew what it meant to have secrets that could hurt your family, so I kept quiet.

I never told Margot the secrets I kept for my own family to protect them. She didn't know that my stepfather was related to my mother, or that my father had given me a boy's name when I was born. Margot didn't know that we grew marijuana beside the outhouse. For all of her probing questions that tested my hidden secrets, I made up lies.

"What are those weird plants in the white buckets?"

"Tomatoes. Hurry up and pee so we can go play," I replied, urging my friend along, while I tried not to notice her nose crinkling at the smell inside the outhouse.

"What's your middle name?"

"I don't have one."

"What do you mean? Everyone has a middle name."

"Well I don't."

"That's weird."

"Why don't you have an indoor toilet?"

"We're getting one soon."

One day, while I was sleeping over, Margot told me about her ghost. By then I had begun to doubt her ability to tell the truth. Margot, it was becoming apparent, liked to tell fantastic tales to see if I would believe her. The mythical princess cousin never materialized, nor was she ever mentioned in the presence of Margot's family, and I eventually began to doubt her existence. Even little things, like stories about how wealthy her family was, or how rare and precious her dolls were, began to appear to me as the over-exaggerations they were to impress me. Still, there was the flutter of belief, or in this case, fear, that some of Margot's fantastic stories held some truth.

While Margot and I huddled under the covers of the double bed in the guest room, we whispered about our classmates at school. As we talked, I tried my best not to look at the many pairs of black eyes staring down at us. This feat was impossible, unless I focused on the bedcovers. Faded faces in the haunting shades of gray and black hung in a horizontal line on every wall, about a foot from the ceiling. We were surrounded by the ghosts of strangers whose eyes never looked away.

"Who are those people in the pictures?" I whispered my question into Margot's ear so they wouldn't hear me.

"I don't know. Dead people I guess."

I was beginning to wish I had not agreed to sleep in this room with Margot, but I didn't want her to know I was afraid. Instead I asked, "How do you know they're dead?"

"Because they're in black-and-white."

I pulled the covers up around my neck and tried to pretend the dead people weren't staring at me, even though I was sure I could feel the heat of their black pupils piercing my skin. "Can we take them down?" I whispered.

"Why, are you scared?" Margot's tone tested and teased.

"No, not really," I lied, "but they look like they're watching us."

"They probably are. You know, my house is haunted. I've seen the ghost. Sometimes when I wake up in the middle of the night it floats across my room." Margot paused, "It goes into my bathroom and never comes out."

My body shivered in response, and I pulled the covers tighter.

Even though my parents told me that ghosts, like God, were not real, that night, under the quilt with Margot, I could not sleep. For the first time I was beginning to doubt my parents' words. What if Margot was right and ghosts really did haunt people's houses? What if I saw hers tonight?

After Margot told me about her ghost, I began to wonder if I would see it someday. Perhaps Margot's specter could travel down the road and visit me at my own house or, worse, maybe my house was haunted too. Although my home was new, up a hill in the woods in back of it there was a place where the ground was sunken and filled with stones from an old foundation. Beside the remains, was a well covered with a gray slab of granite. Whenever I would walk by these two holes in the ground I would imagine a family who had once lived there. A family now dead, their remains spread beneath the stones of the foundation, with one unfortunate child trapped under the rock covering the well. Each time I would pass by this sunken pile of rocks, my body would shiver with the possibility of what lurked beneath.

Once, when I was nine, I walked into my room and thought I saw the shadow of a spirit glide across the floor. At school the next day I told Margot, who laughed in return. "You're only saying that because my house is haunted," she told me, flashing our friend Jill a knowing smile.

Days later when I saw the same shadow glide across the floor, then looked up to see the flutter of plastic wrap settling back over my science project of chloroformed butterflies, my heart sank with relief. I didn't tell Margot she was right.

Even if real ghosts were not lurking inside of my house, the ghosts of my family's secrets and my mother's stories always haunted my presence. Along with her stories of the physical and emotional abuse she endured in the earlier years of her life, my mother began sharing with me and Tara stories about sexual abuse. These tales, like the others, began to tuck their way into the folds of my body, nestling deep into my cells where they created tissues filled with fear.

"My mother was an illegitimate child," she told us. "Stauvik was not her real father." "You know Stauvik was a pedophile," my mother revealed. "He used to molest my mother when she was a child."

In my mind I thought of the great-grandparents I barely knew, and of the few times I had been to their home before Stauvik passed away. I thought of Starka, my great-grandmother, and how she made beautiful crochet dresses for dolls. My mind traveled to their kitchen, where I would watch, with anticipation, the cuckoo clock announce the hour. I tried not to think of Stauvik and how I had played inside his house before he died.

"Stauvik molested my brother too," my mother continued, "when my grandparents would babysit him."

"That's why he's so messed up."

While my mother spoke, I thought, *What about me. What about us? Did anyone ever touch us? Did he, or anyone else ever molest me or Tara?* My body held the uncomfortable feeling that these things had also happened to me, even though my mind could not conjure a definitive memory.

"He never messed with me," my mother added. "Only Ben."

73

Paranoia grew inside of me with my mother's stories. Bad things, I was sure, could happen if I wasn't careful. I became hyper-vigilant and aware. At night, before I allowed myself to settle into sleep, my eyes darted to the dark corners of my room, and just out-side the door into the shadows of the hallway. Back and forth I would look, three times, before I was sure nothing was there. Then, quickly, I dove under my blankets, and tucked the top edges around my head as I turned my eyes away from what I could not see.

There were dark shadows in the daytime, too. The forest was full of them, and so was the road from the elementary school to my home. Some days, when our parents wrote us permission notes, I would walk home from school with Margot, or my sister. When I was with Margot, we skipped happily along the side of the road, gossiping and giggling until we reached the end of Margot's drive-way. After I left my best-friend at her mailbox, I felt the dark press of the trees, and my mind conjured specters among the brown shad-ows, and kidnappers lurking behind rocks on the roadsides. For the last quarter-mile I ran.

One day, but it could have been a dream, I heard the slow crunch of dirt chewed by the treads of tires behind me as I walked home with my sister. We had just passed Margot's house, and Tara and I were making our way up the small rise of a hill before our mailbox came into view. There were no other houses between our home and Margot's, and with that crunch of tires that did not pass, my heart began to panic, pounding its alarm down to my feet. When I turned to my sister, the fear I felt was mirrored in her face.

Without speaking we began to run, stopping to the sound of si-lence at the top of the hill. Turning around, we discovered the car that had been following us was now stationary, its doors opened to two laughing men who were each putting one foot upon the ground. Before my own feet found flight, I looked into their faces. The man on the left seemed too familiar, with his busy brown hair and eyes shaped like mine. Without words, I turned to my sister and together we ran, taking a short-cut through the woods, our feet refusing to stop until we were safe behind the closed door of our home. We never looked back.

Many years later I asked my sister if she remembered this day. "I don't even remember walking home from school," she told me.

"We used to sometimes when we had permission notes," I told her, trying to jolt her memory. "And, I used to walk home with Margot once in a while."

"Well anyway," I added, "I have always wondered if that memory of the car was really a dream."

I was disappointed, though. This scene, which had stayed with me like that day at Hampton beach my sister does not remember, seemed too real to be imagined. For a long time I believed that one of the men who had followed us home that day was our father, traveling three thousand miles across the country with a friend to kidnap us. It became an irrational fear that lingered in my mind and in my body.

Alone

see
a daughter
cross the sky
She said
I had no choice

I remember words
they

are folded
in my stomach

In December of 1981, Tara and I flew to Oregon for Christmas. It was the first of our court-ordered visits with our father. We were eight and nine-years-old. The day we left, my mother and stepfather drove us to the airport in Boston, Massachusetts to see us off. I sometimes wonder what it was like for my mother to place her two young daughters on a plane, sending them three thousand miles across the sky, to stay in the care of a man she did not like or trust. She once said to me when we spoke of these trips, "It was a strange feeling as a mother, but I had no choice."

"Take care of each other," my mother said before Tara and I followed a stewardess onto the plane.

After my sister and I were buckled into our seats, the same stewardess gave each of us a deck of cards with TWA on the cover, along with two folded blankets, and two white pillows so we could sleep after we ate our dinner. When our meals arrived I tried my best to swallow my food, but already the knots in my stomach had begun to form. With each bite, another knot tied, and finally I handed my tray to the stewardess who asked me if I was all set. I nodded, then leaned my head against the window, cushioned by my pillow.

Closing my eyes to sleep was impossible. Unable to endure the pain in my stomach any longer, I whispered into my sister's ear that I felt sick, and that I thought I might throw-up. I remember Tara's pause when I told her I was ill. On her face I saw her struggle with the annoyance of a little sister who was unwell, and the fear and concern that comes with a responsibility that is beyond one's years.

Tara's concern for me won, and she pulled her courage into her legs and throat to seek out the stewardess who returned with a small cup of liquid and told me to drink it down. An hour later I awoke next to my sister, whose face softened into relief.

We arrived at Portland International Airport before the sun rose. Waiting to welcome us, were my father, Grammie, my grandmother and Poppy, and my mother's youngest brother. Outside the airport doors, a small black limousine was parked, with a chauffeur in a black cap standing beside it. In his hand he held two red roses.

Feeling tired and thunderstruck after the flight, I hugged my relatives and my father, whose eyes wore the sheen of joy. As we headed outside, I zipped my second-hand parka against the chill of winter, and gazed with confusion at the black car in front of the building, with a strange man smiling beside it.

"Go ahead, get inside," my father told us. "We're taking a limo to Grammie's."

Grammie's Christmas gifts, along with those from our father, were waiting for us when we got to her house, wrapped in shiny red and green paper beneath the Christmas tree. Grammie lived in an old, large white colonial in Portland with my father and one of my uncles. My paternal grandfather had passed away eight years earlier, from a heart attack, six months after my birth.

The first presents my sister and I unwrapped that night at Grammie's revealed folded satin in the form of pajamas. Well, perhaps it was not satin, but to my eight-year-old eyes it was. The cloth of my pajamas was pale pink, like the tips of apple blossoms. It unfolded into a rippling nightgown with short, puffed sleeves. Beneath the nightgown, in the box, was a long robe made of matching pink satin. Grammie also gave us skirts for the holiday, which looked like fancy wrapping paper pattered in shiny red and green plaid. She edged them in ruffles, and when I spun my skirt the next morning, it rippled in waves of Christmas around my waist. The last gift I opened, the size of a shoe box, held the prettiest doll I had ever seen. The first in my collection of Effanbee Story Book dolls, the Sugar Plum Fairy dressed in pink and lace.

Later, when I slipped into my nightgown and covered it with the robe before I nestled into one of Grammie's spare beds, I was sure I knew what it felt like to be a real princess. I hoped my sister, sleeping beside me, was not disappointed that her satin was sky blue and separated into a top and pants, without a matching robe.

Tara and I slept in a room covered in pink and blue roses, and hung with old pictures in frames. I loved this room, and all of Grammie's house, which was stuffed with antiques filmed in dust. In the living room there was a large wooden spinning wheel that I turned softly with my hands when Grammie was out of sight, and a piano that played sheets of music with punched holes as though through the invisible hands of a ghost. On the far end of the room, French doors opened into a large rectangular closet filled with toys for the grandkids.

"Don't touch the dollhouse," Grammie told us when we opened the glass doors to the room. "You might break the furniture." Instead of playing with the dollhouse, I gazed with longing at the miniature rooms filled with tiny beds and dressers. My eyes traveling to the kitchen with its black stove topped with a silver tea kettle. Around a table, a family of four, miniature-sized, waited to be served.

Treasures could be found throughout Grammie's house, and some of them we were allowed to play with. Six old-fashioned gumball machines stood at attention around her dining-room table, and each was filled with a rainbow of treats. With a nickel we could buy the sweet drop of a rainbow and roll its color on our tongues.

In Grammie's kitchen, where she loved to cook big meals for family gatherings, copper pans hung from the walls, and turquoise canisters lined its shelves. Fake flowers in vases adorned tables, and old fashioned ladies wearing glamorous hats and long dresses with cinched waists hung from the walls of her hallways and bedrooms. In their white gloved hands they held skinny cigarettes against red lips. Just like the cigarettes Grammie smoked outside in her rose garden. All of Grammie's treasures were wonderful to my child-eyes, no matter how dusty they were.

In the evenings, Grammie often worked as a waitress at a Mexican restaurant called Ponchos. During that week, as we would each summer that followed it, we ate a dinner at Ponchos while Grammie was waitressing. While I sat at our table, I gazed at the white adobe walls hung with Mexico, and waited for Grammie to arrive with my tostada salad and Shirley Temple. Grammie's face, when she delivered my plate, shined with pleasure as she winked, then whispered in my ear, "Here you go Leethe," before she handed me a cup filled with maraschino cherries.

On the nights when she worked, Grammie would return home late, and I would wake the next morning to find her still asleep on the sofa in the living room, with a crocheted afghan wrapped around her body. Beside her, stuck to the surface of the coffee table, were her paste-on lashes looking like the plucked wings of fairies.

One morning, while she was still asleep, I peeled the black fringes off the table and pasted them on the top of each of my eyelids. Grammie was not pleased when she woke and saw her lashes on my eyes, "Take those off," she told me, forgetting to add "Leethe" to her reprimand.

Instead of sleeping in it, Grammie used the space in her bedroom to store her abundance of clothing. Shirts and dresses, still tagged, hung from the doors of her closet and draped their fancy fabrics over the sides of her bed. Grammie loved to shop, and one day, during our week's stay, she took me and Tara with her to the nearby "sample stores" in her gray Audi. It was the only time we had Grammie all to ourselves.

At the sample stores, the three of us sorted through racks and piles of department store castoffs, filling our shopping cart with new blouses, skirts and pants for school. Most of the clothing I selected with Grammie matched my sister's, which made Tara roll her eyes. She didn't make me put it back, though.

The rest of the week, aside from an overnight at our maternal grandparents, Tara and I spent taking drives with our father. One of the things I remember most about being with our father is driving through the beautiful expanse of Oregon squished together in the front seat of his truck without seat belts. In my memory, they were long drives, the air in the small cab filled with a collective, quiet unease. When our father tried to engage us in conversation, he didn't complain like Keith did when Tara and I gave him one-word answers. Instead of probing for information, he most often started talking about himself.

"I told you," our mother said in confirmation of her belief after we returned to New Hampshire, "he only cares about himself."

Six months later, Tara and I flew west to visit our father for one month. Once again, instead of finding out about how we were doing in school, who are friends were, what sports we liked to play, what books we liked to read, and how our life was with the man who had replaced him, our father talked about himself. He told us about the ivy he was waging a battle against on the roadsides, the new exhibits he was working on at the zoo, and how much it cost him to fly us out, get us swimming lessons, and feed us for the month.

"I was always hungry," my sister recalls about being with a parent who didn't seem to understand the needs of a growing child.

I remember the uncomfortable curve of the Oregon highways, and the tension of my body as it tried not to rock against my father's while sitting sandwiched between him and my sister. When we drove the hour to the zoo to spend the day where my father worked, his demeanor relaxed into a habitual comfort supplemented by pride. With his keys in hand, he led us through the backdoors of not-yet-open exhibits, pointing out the vegetation he had planted along the way. Tara and I, in turn, feigned interest, as we did with our stepfather and his building projects.

Being the daughters of a zoo employee had its privileges, though. Keys unlocked back doors of cages, and we walked with eager anticipation up the steps of the giraffe enclosure with carrots in hand. As I felt the thick bluish tongue of the giraffe brush my hand, I realized the privileges that can come with being an insider.

There were also downfalls to having my father work at the zoo. At lunch, during our first visit to the zoo that summer, our father took us to the break-room, where dozens of employees were gathered, camouflaging together in their beige attire, to eat.

"These are my girls, Tara and Alethea," my father announced to the full room, whose faces turned toward his proud words.

"They're beautiful," a woman we didn't know nodded our way before she spooned yogurt into her mouth.

"Wow, they've sure grown," a man I was sure I'd never seen before spanned the length of our bodies with his eyes. I blushed, and turned my head down.

The coworker closest to us, extended his right hand, and Tara and I took turns placing our hands in his grasp. "Nice to meet you," I mumbled my response as I looked into the eyes of another stranger, my face blazing with heat.

In those long minutes, standing in the break-room, my head filled with the voices of my stepfather, "I'm your father now," and my mother, "He never cared about you girls." Their words flamed the uncomfortable fire growing inside of me.

Later that evening, we ate dinner outside, under the trees where the shadows cast by a setting sun shivered my body. Another moment in time that would become permanently lodged within my cellular memories.

"So," my father lets out a nervous cough. I am nearly finished chewing my last bite of food. "You girls need to figure out what you want to call me."

With his words, my heart begins a wild skip inside of my chest before it jumps into my throat to block my voice. My father looks past our empty cans of pop, first at my sister, then at me. He is waiting for us to speak; to answer the question he has asked. The first one to open her mouth, I know, will declare the loser of a battle that cannot be won. Frustration and anger builds inside of me. No one has prepared us for this moment. Words swirl into confusion inside my mind.

Although I would rather look away, I search my father's face for an answer, but I can't find one amid the shadowy play of pines across his skin. Instead, I see a man who is almost a stranger, with a forehead pulled tight into lines that deepen with the darkness of trees.

Inside of his eyes, brown shadows mix into green, like a murky pond. Within each center I can see a picture of myself captured below the surface. I appear small, trapped in their dark wells. I don't like this mirror. It is not where I want to be found. My eyes turn down, past his lips, which are pulled into a double line without a space. I follow the frayed edges of the quilt, where we sit, to study the orange needles scattered beside our island of cloth, and allow myself to become absorbed by their complexity; the way they layer to add depth and light to the forest floor.

Above my head, my father's mouth opens again, and I hear his words repeated, an echo coming back to me.

"What do you girls want to call me? You can't just call me nothing." The last words feel like a knife, and I realize my father is not as stupid as my mother has led me to believe. Tara and I have struggled to avoid using a name to define him, and he has noticed.

83

Still, Tara and I do not answer, and I fidget on the blanket, wishing for a place to disappear. Inside of my mind, I see the face of my stepfather, stern and unwavering. "Call *me* dad now," I hear the echo of his words. Over his sullen and disappointed face, I see the first books I ever wrote, from first grade. Their wallpapered covers open to reveal typed words crossed out by my hand in black marker. Corrections made after I proudly displayed my stories to my mother and stepfather. Now the words of my mother fill my mind. "You hurt dad's feelings by saying you have two fathers." I think of how, after my mother took me upstairs to tell me this, I took a marker from my desk and put a black line through the word "two" and substituted it with the word "one" before I replaced, with an over-sized period, the "s" at the end of the word "dad," in each book.

How can I tell the father before me, I wonder, that he's already been permanently replaced? I don't know what to say. I don't want to get it wrong again. So I wait for him to give me the answer, and finally he does.

"It's fine," he says with a face that makes me turn away, "if you want to call me Dave."

The first time I speak the name Dave, it catches in my throat. The second, knots with the first. By the fifteenth, there is a bundle of knotted letters, lodged like a brick.

***

On the flight home to New Hampshire that summer, I had my first taste of meat. The stewardess, not knowing we were vegetarians, served me and my sister a complete country breakfast of scrambled eggs, sausage and toast. Tara, immediately alarmed by the links of pork nestled beside our eggs, warned me not to touch the glistening meat. She also made the mistake of going to the bathroom before our breakfasts were finished.

While my sister was in the lavatory, I stared hard at those brown steaming links. Their succulent smell was too much to bear. My stomach grumbled its plea, and my mouth dripped with moisture. More than anything at that moment, I wanted those sausages. By the time Tara returned to her seat, not only were mine gone, but hers had disappeared as well into my satisfied stomach. My sister, when she saw the missing links from our trays, turned to me in horror.

"You ate the sausages!" she cried out as though I had just picked and consumed not one, but four, poisonous mushrooms (In a way, I suppose, I had.).

"Mom and dad are going to kill you!"

"I don't care," I replied. "They were delicious!"

Tara held the secret of my crime just until we made it through the arrival gates and into the arms of our waiting mother and stepfather. Instead of the cries of alarm she had anticipated, our parents erupted into laughter.

"How'd they taste?" my stepfather asked me with a wink of his eye.

Block the voice

forever whispering inside my head

ask me about
silence
We weren't supposed to talk
ask
me

about
guilt
trying to eat our

Truth

When I was a child, my maternal grandparents lived on the top of Mt. Scott, over-looking the city of Portland, Oregon, in a house where Lysol reigned. To say my grandmother kept a clean house would be an understatement. When we walked inside the door, the air cleared, and our shoes disappeared before they could reach the fern-green carpet of the living room. I loved my grandparents' living room with its soft floor and furry silver chairs that swiveled under my restless body. When the sun descended upon the yellow-and-blue flowers of their couches, Tara, and I would sometimes make a bed upon the carpet, using thin mattresses covered with sheets to sleep amid the deep green shadows of our silent forest.

Each time I visited, I clung to the clean surfaces of my grandparents' home and its perfect order, and tried to block out the unpleasant memories of my mother's stories. When I settled into the comforts of being a grandchild, I was almost always happy and content. As grandparents, my mother's parents were loving and kind. Never did Poppy raise a hand towards us in punishment, and rarely did his voice reach past the point of indulgence. My grandmother, in turn, indulged us with all the forbidden foods we were not allowed at home, complimented Tara and me on how we were turning out, and told us amusing stories about our mother when she was young.

"You girls have such pretty hands," my grandmother would saw said as she rubbed her fingers softly over my skin when I asked her to file my nails like hers. "Remember to push back your cuticles so you can see your moons."

"You and Tara are so pretty, you look just like your mom when she was little," my grandmother would remark as we flipped through her photo albums.

"Your mother was a little wild, though," she'd laugh. "I never quite knew what she was up to and whether she was looking for trouble."

"One day when your momma was, oh, maybe around ten-years-old, the boy next door came over to visit and asked your mom what she was doing. She and Jane had just finished painting, and your mother took her cup of water that she had been using to clean their brushes and told that boy that it was Kool-Aid. He didn't know your mom was bluffing and he drank it down. Boy did your mom ever think that was funny!"

"When she was a teenager, she sure was popular. Look at how pretty your mom was," my grandmother would say, pointing to my mother's senior class picture. "She had more boyfriends... I never knew who was coming or going out the front door."

As my grandmother spoke her memories about my mother, I would giggle as my heart swelled with pride for my beautiful, mischievous mother.

Sometimes, though, while we were seated around the kitchen table for a meal, my grandmother would ask me and Tara questions about life back home. Questions that made me squirm with discomfort.

"How's Keith doing?"

"You mean our *dad*?" Either Tara or I would correct her out of loyalty. "He's fine."

"That's good. How are his parents? Have you seen them recently?"

"They're good," Then we might add some proof, such as, "They had a going-away party for us before we left."

"Oh, that's nice."

"Yeah."

"So Keith is being good to you girls?"

"Yes."

Mostly, we answered our grandmother's questions with as few words as possible, trying to make our life appear normal and fine. Each summer, before we left for our trips to Oregon, my mother would caution us, "Don't talk about our life here. It's none of their business. My mother is nosey and she'll just twist your words." My grandparents, as a result, never knew about the tepee in Henniker, the marijuana plants tucked beside the stream, how many years we spent without indoor bathrooms, the stern control of our stepfather, or about the many ways we felt like we did not belong in our stepfamily. They never knew how much we missed and needed their loving presence in our lives, because Tara and I did our best to pretend we were living a near-perfect childhood in New Hampshire with a loving father who had replaced the one who didn't really want us.

My grandmother intuited enough to know that Tara and I were learning to dislike the father we were obligated to visit each summer. Sometimes she would probe us for answers as to why, though, and her words would fill my stomach with an uncomfortable mix of guilt and confusion. "You know he really misses you girls. It's really hard on him that you live so far away," she would say as we tried to enjoy our sugared cereal at breakfast. When I lifted my eyes from my bowl to her face, I felt as though my beloved grandmother's eyes were testing me.

As my grandmother spoke, the discomfort inside of me squirmed for release. Questions found homes inside my mind, but I never gave them a voice. If my grandmother was right, my inner voice asked, was my mother wrong? If my grandmother was right, why didn't my father fight harder to keep us? Why didn't he fly out to see us more often? Why didn't he send my mother enough child-support? Why didn't he tell us how much he wanted us to come home? And, why did my grandmother think this was, in some way, my fault and Tara's? Weren't we just doing what our mother told us to?

My body tensed with defense, and my lips closed to words. I wanted only to eat and feel love here, in my grandparents' house. And eat we did. If you opened the cabinets of my grandmother's kitchen you would find perfect rows of cereal in at least ten different boxes, some with sugared rings and flakes. Cereal we never ate at home. On another shelf sat red canisters of Pringles, shiny bags of Doritos, glass jars of home-dried Granny Smith apples, and cans of salted nuts. A pull-out drawer beside the oven opened into bags of Hersey Kisses and Reese's Peanut Butter Cups. And if we went downstairs, into the cool gray of the basement room beside the garage, we would find stacked in six-packs, cans of pop. It was a hippie child's Nirvana. Nothing was forbidden.

Except dirt. Which I am sure we brought in on our sweaty bodies; tiny clods slipping from our bare feet as we raced from the pool, across the lawn, turning cartwheels before we galloped through the sliding doors for another can of lemon-lime Slice. We never saw it, though. Our grime disappeared beneath my grandmother's vacuum, and with a swift swipe of a white paper towel across her counters.

When the air was warm and the sky blue, we would swim with our cousins in the chlorinated waters of our grandparents' pool. If I breathe deeply, I can still smell the sun-soaked chips of cedar mixed with the sweet blue-green of juniper surrounding the pool deck. I can almost feel the deep lines on my thighs imprinted by the rubbery vinyl of the lounge chairs where we would sit, drying in the sun, eating handfuls of curled chips and sweet withered apples.

At night, before bed, Tara and I would bathe in the white porcelain of my grandparents' bathtub, popping rainbow-colored balls of soap out of the glass jar beside the tub. My hands remember the squish of delight as their pearlized forms burst to color the gush of water from the faucet. Our tanned bodies glistened new inside the bath-full of bubbles while we washed the day's grime away. Later, when I said goodnight to Poppy, he would kiss gently the clean skin of my forehead. When my grandmother tucked me into bed, I willed my mind to forget my mother's stories.

Nutmeg

I recall

years of
detachment

Guilt burrowing deep inside
my heart
to save her

remember
love

The winter after my mother married Keith, she completed her nursing degree at a local technical college. With my mother now working outside of the home, my sister and I spent the following summer largely in the care of other people.

Some days, my mother would pack lunches for my stepfather, Tara and me, and the three of us would head off together to spend the day at his worksite. I remember one place in particular. My stepfather was renovating an old white farmhouse surrounded by stone-walled fields. Tara and I tried to while away the long hours of our day with him by exploring acres of long grasses, and visiting sheep that grazed the fields. At noon we would meet up with our stepfather and eat lunch together. When we opened our lunch boxes we searched first for the small squares of paper my mother had tucked under our sandwiches. I still have one of them, glued into a page of my childhood scrapbook. On the piece of notepaper my mother had written this poem for me:

Roses are red
Violets are blue
If I had those cheeks
I'd feel pretty neat

I cherished these simple poems, reading my mother's love inside their neatly printed words. I knew Tara and my stepfather looked forward to their poems too, but it wasn't easy for the three of us to spend those long days together. Tara and I didn't always agree with how to use our time, and we often argued out of boredom. My stepfather, in turn, seemed perpetually disappointed by our lack of interest in his occupation, and by our silence at lunchtime and during the long drives in his truck to and from his job sites.

"So what did you girls do today? Did you see anything interesting?" he'd ask on the way home.

Tara and I would look at each other, until finally one of us offered a few words. "We went to see the sheep."

"What else?"

"Um, we read our books."

There would be a long awkward silence, and then the guilt. "You girls should be able to carry on a conversation with me while we're in the car. We shouldn't have to drive in silence. Why don't you ask me about my day? You know, show some interest in my life too."

A knot of constriction would now have formed between my throat and my chest. I was pretty sure Tara had one too, as it was always difficult for us to ask our stepfather about himself. Not only did we not really care about his work, which we thought was boring, whatever we said never seemed to be enough.

"Well I've got a new job site that I'm starting next week," my stepfather might interject to fill our silence. "I told your mom I'd take us all out to see it this weekend."

I tried my best to muster a molecule of enthusiasm, while my heart sank with the chore of visiting yet another one of my stepfather's worksites. "That's great, um, what are you going to be working on?" I managed to squeak the question out.

If I was convincing enough, or Tara, if she was the one talking, our stepfather would launch into the details of his new job and fill the silence between us for several minutes. Tara and I, now able to breathe a little more freely, would gaze once again out the windows of the truck and think about other things.

We preferred the days we spent with our sitter, a sixteen-year-old girl named Naomi who lived in a large farmhouse house with her mother and three sisters, about a mile-and-a-half from our home. On sunny days the three of us would bike back and forth between our two houses. Tara and I loved being with Naomi, especially when we visited her big home full of teenaged sisters. Bedrooms filled with tapestries and beads blasted rock music through open doors, and someone was always on the phone talking to a boyfriend. That summer one of Naomi's sisters was dating Keith's youngest brother, a fact I found delightful.

"Maybe she'll marry him," I told Naomi. "Then we'd be related."

"Maybe," she laughed. "Who knows."

One hot day, Naomi drove me and Tara to Hampton Beach in her tiny yellow car to swim in the cool salted waters of the Atlantic. Together we spent the day swimming, sunbathing and walking the boardwalk to get ice cream and play arcades. Tara didn't get lost, and no one tried to swing us over the waves. It was a fabulous day.

It was the same summer we got Nutmeg. One day my stepfather announced that we could maybe, just maybe get a puppy. Like most children, Tara and thought we wanted a dog.

"Someone I know has a litter of mutts in Northfield. I told your mom we could go and have a look at them this weekend."

Tara and I turned to each other in disbelief. Before us was a man who had always complained about other people's dogs. A man who seemed to have no use for these smelly, barking beasts.

"Really?"

"Of course. I wouldn't have suggested it if I didn't mean it."

Tara and I chose a fawn-colored puppy with a black nose, and ears that looked like they were dipped in soot. My mother named her Nutmeg, and Tara, my stepfather and I set to work building a home for our new pet. It was the only project on which the three of us willingly worked towards the finished result.

The dog house was a fine home, constructed solidly out of plywood with insulated walls and a shingled roof. It had just enough room for an adult dog to lie down comfortably inside. When it was finished, we placed Nutmeg's house under the pines behind our home, half-way down the lane leading to the outhouse, and strung a runner between two trees. This soon became Nutmeg's permanent home.

It was almost easy to forget we had a dog after Nutmeg was old enough to live outside. Within a few weeks of having her, our new pet became an out-door-only dog, and our cats resumed their free reign of the household.

"She's your dog, girls," our stepfather told us. "You're responsible for feeding her and giving her water."

No one, though, taught us how to train her, and soon Nutmeg learned to escape when we let her loose. Twice we got a call from the police department telling us that Nutmeg had followed a jogger and we needed to pay a fine to retrieve her.

"That dog needs to stay on the leash or runner," our stepfather would remind us. "We can't keep picking her up from the station."

Once in a while, my mother, Tara and I would bring Nutmeg to a secluded forest pond. Here, Nutmeg would be allowed to run and swim with abandon, jumping with pleasure off the rocks with us into the dark, cool water.

After Nutmeg's residence was permanently moved outside, Tara and I began to lose interest in her. Instead of visiting with our dog on her runner under the pines, we preferred to play with our cats, who were allowed to sleep on our beds and cuddle with us on the couch. It became more of a chore than a pleasure for me to go outside every day and pet Nutmeg, and to deliver her food and water. Nutmeg, who would greet me with a wagging tail, eager for affection, made me feel guilty. It was not what I had imagined life with a dog would be like.

Three years after we got her, my stepfather decided it would be best to relinquish Nutmeg to the SPCA. Although I never developed the attachment to Nutmeg that I had for my cats, I was filled with turmoil about letting her go. My parents, when they sat us down at the kitchen table to discuss her fate, didn't sugar-coat her probable fate.

"Will she find a new home?" I asked.

My mother looked at my stepfather, who responded. "Maybe, Alethea, but since she's an adult dog, and there are a lot of adult dogs who are brought there, there's a good chance she'll be put to sleep."

"It's the best thing," my mother added after she looked at my face. "She's always running off, and she doesn't have much of a life on that runner."

"You girls don't even pay any attention to her," my stepfather said, compounding the weight of guilt that was growing inside of me.

That night, in the privacy of my bed, I prayed with a silent fervor, to a god I was not sure I believed in, that a wonderful family would go to the shelter and take Nutmeg home. I prayed that they would give her the love and attention we were never able to, and that finally she would have a good life. My heart was heavy with the weight that we had not loved Nutmeg enough to keep her.

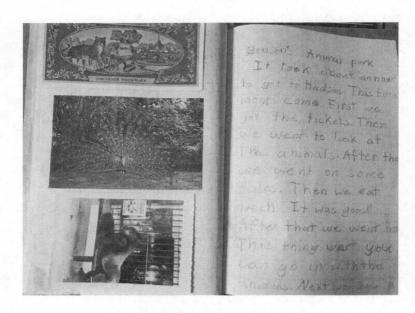

The journal I saved

carefully
catalogued
adventures in a blue notebook
not optional

statistics
count minutes. lines
recall
the pattern of corrections

Upon closer study
see
my attempt to separate out me

My step-grandparents had a large oval island in the center of their kitchen. The island was covered in veined green granite and bordered with maple shelves. In the front, facing the living room, the shelves were enclosed by panes of glass that showcased my step-grandmother's treasured china. Among these pieces was a blue-and-white floral tea set meant for a small child. I wanted to be that child. Sometimes, with permission, I would open the clear doors and peer at the miniature plates and cups, letting my fingers graze the glossy edges of the porcelain while I imagined grand parties where I served tiny iced cakes and tea with a splash of milk and a sprinkle of sugar.

I doubt my step-grandmother knew how much I coveted her tea-set, which seemed to wait patiently for a child's hands to love it again. I never told her or anyone else how much I wanted that tea set to be mine. Perhaps, if I had asked, my step-grandmother would have given it to me, but I never felt worthy of it. Instead, I was sure the set would be passed down to the first of her real granddaughters to ask for it.

I didn't ask for things from my step-grandparents, but tried graciously to accept whatever was offered. In the seventh grade, my step-grandmother gave me her ancient alpine skis, which she had replaced with a new set. I took them with a mixture of regret and gratitude, worried about the teasing remarks from my peers. Thankfully, I only had to use them for one year.

Usually for Christmas, my step-grandmother would give Tara and me ski tickets, and she would take us skiing during our winter vacation. Keith's mother, who was a good cook, would pack enormous lunches in her Igloo cooler. While we warmed in the lodge at noontime, we'd munch on chips, deviled eggs, pickles and sandwiches, and she would tell us about skiing with her boys when they were young, down the small hill beside their childhood home. The brothers were the envy of the town, owning the bragging rights of having the only ski hill in town, equipped with a rope-tow and a large warming hut. To me, it sounded like a wonderful childhood.

When we weren't talking about school, or her boys when they were young, the three of us would sometimes sing harmonies while we drove. Songs that we often sang during the summer of 1982 when my step-grandmother took us on weekly outings across New Hampshire. My step-grandmother would lead a song with her confident soprano, "Oooo, mares eat oats and does eat oats and little lambs eat ivy, a kid'll eat ivy too, wouldn't you?!" Tara and I would shyly join in by the second refrain, our quiet, off-key voices becoming louder until we gradually harmonized without care of how we sounded to the world outside our windows. Our step-grandmother, unlike her son, never commented upon the dissonance of our voices.

I'd like to believe the three of us enjoyed much of our time together during the summer of 1982, when my step-grandmother decided she would take us to a different local landmark each week. An educator by profession, Keith's mother often looked for an opportunity to add to our personal edification. Before we began our first outing together, she handed me a blue journal, and my sister a green.

"These are for you girls to record our trips. I'd like you to write about each one, and then show me after you are done." When our step-grandmother handed them back to us before our next adventure together, they came marked with her edits. Tara and I wrote in pencil so we could correct our mistakes.

My step-grandmother took me and Tara on seven day trips that summer, and each excursion was carefully catalogued in the form of an essay in my blue notebook. Beside some of them I pasted postcards and admissions tickets to commemorate the day.

Our first trip together was to the Isles of Shoals off the coast of Portsmouth, New Hampshire. During the boat ride, I looked for whales and seals, and took note of the time it took to travel to land. In my essay, I quote statistics: how long it took to get to Portsmouth, "about an hour," how many passengers the Viking Sun could hold, "five hundred," and the duration of the tour of Star Island, "1:15." It seems I was always counting minutes during our trips together, which were like my school field trips, only smaller. With one teacher and two students, there was no way to blend into a crowd. When I was bored, I did my best to feign interest and to stay alert. I knew I had to learn something from each outing, as there was always the test in the end, in the form of my journal entry.

There are three lines in the middle of my essay to the Isles of Shoals that have the smudges of an eraser. After noting my spelling and grammatical errors, my step-grandmother would hand me back the journal for our next outing together. I dreaded this part of our adventures. Journaling became a chore and a lesson, instead of a private musing of thoughts. It was a task that lurked in my mind in wait, while I tried to enjoy our time together.

I found myself comparing my step-grandmother, who insisted that Tara and I call her "grandma," to my friends' grandmothers. As I listened to my friends recount weekends spent going into Boston or the movies, then sleeping over at their grandparents' houses, I couldn't help missing my grandparents on top of Mt. Scott in Oregon. When Tara and spent an overnight at her house, we often vacuumed her floors, helped my grandmother with dishes and laundry, and once in a while our step-grandfather would bring us to the center store and buy us an ice cream bar.

When I look back through the journal, and the photographs in the album from my mother that were taken during these day trips with my step-grandmother, I feel the memory of my emotions still lodged inside of my body. In my upper belly there is the echo of excitement from seeing the black head of a seal pop above the waves on the way to the Isles of Shoals. My heart remembers the quickening of its beat when I dove down a waterslide. My tongue, the sweet buttery taste of my favorite ice cream. Deep in my belly and in my throat, though, I feel the constriction of conditional love.

Conditions

Show A Different World
made together

boldly clear of
the piercing dissonance of
power
learn to love a
new

Truth

After my family moved to Canterbury, we slowly shed our hippie lifestyle, one aspect at a time. I was in the second or third grade when we got an indoor toilet. A year or two later, my stepfather stopped growing marijuana beside the outhouse, which he preferred to use as a toilet long after we got a bathroom inside. Around the time Keith installed our indoor toilet, he brought home a second-hand black-and-white TV, and sat it on a homemade shelf in the corner of the room next to our kitchen table, and across from our wrap-around wooden couch.

Both the TV and the indoor toilet came with conditions. "You can watch three shows a week," our stepfather told me and Tara. "On the weekends and only at night. No TV during the day." Most of the shows, approved by our stepfather, were on PBS. After he replaced the TV with a colored one, and the "Cosby Show" and "A Different World" started airing on a commercial network, my stepfather made an exception to his rule. On Thursday nights at 8:00 p.m., the four of us would squish together on our home-made L-shaped couch. My stepfather always sat in the coveted corner spot with leg room with my mother beside him. Tara and I crammed together in the remaining space, with our knees to our chests, trying our best not to touch each other too much. If I got the side spot, I could lean against the curved wooden slats and position my elbow on my bent knee to create a shield with my hand, blocking my stepfather from my peripheral vision.

During our hour together, in between laughs, my stepfather cleared the mucus from his throat. I, in turn, sat in the corner and cringed. Sometimes, when I became over-whelmed with irritation, I offered an echo from my own throat. Never too loudly, and my stepfather appeared not to notice that I was mocking him with my disgust.

105

My stepfather's chronic throat-clearing irritated me only slightly more than his whistling, which he often did when he was happy. Like when he sang, my stepfather whistled with confident enthusiasm, seemingly oblivious to the dissonance it created in the ears around him. I had no retort for the whistling, except avoidance as best I could. Retreating to my bedroom muffled the sound, but not entirely, as the bedroom doors, like the bathroom door, were never closed.

"What are you trying to hide?" my stepfather asked if we attempted to shut ourselves in a room. He, in turn, paraded his body from his bedroom into our shared bathroom, quite frequently, naked. I learned avoidance when the water for the shower started to run.

I could not, though, turn away from his embraces. This, I knew, would only make him feel unloved and angry. Nightly kisses were made on the lips, and when he was feeling particularly amorous, Keith would place his mouth on the backs of our necks: my mother's, Tara's, and mine. "Your skin is so soft," he'd tell us upon release, and the recoil in my body would slowly relax.

Impertinence was rare. I feared my stepfather's volatility above anything else, and tried my best to avoid igniting his anger. My infrequent moments of disrespect occurred most often at the dinner table, where the four of us would sit together every evening and discuss the day's events. "What did you do in school today?" my stepfather would ask us over our plates of tofu and rice, or pasta topped with chunky home-made sauce.

Usually I had a readily prepared answer, knowing this nightly question was coming, but sometimes it was not good enough.

"Alethea, speak louder," my stepfather would say. "Articulate your answer. I can't hear you." Or, "What else did you do at school? What did you get on your spelling test?"

Our schooling was never confined to the classroom. While his mother was adding to our personal edification during our day-trips together, our stepfather came up with the idea that Tara and I should read the newspaper and present current-event synopses at the dinner table. Dinner became a chore that I couldn't wait to be through with. When I was not presenting my current-event, I tried to block my ears from my stepfather's noisy eating and throat-clearing, while trying to make sure I stayed alert to his inevitable questions.

Sometimes, exasperation or annoyance would flare inside of me and I'd find myself rolling my eyes, or tainting my answers with sass. "I don't know," I'd tell him if he demanded more from me, or "I can't remember." If my stepfather was feeling kind, he'd shout back, "Excuse me. What did you say?" If he allowed his anger to fuel, my stepfather's right hand would shoot across the table and form a vise around my throat.

Tara, more boldly and more often, challenged our stepfather. By the time she was a teenager, the two of them engaged in arguments that made me silently cheer for my sister, while fearing for her safety. My stepfather stopped using his hands to control Tara when she was seventeen. That day Tara's best-friend, Jackie was over. The two girls were getting ready to go out together. Before Tara and Jackie got into the car, our stepfather stopped Tara, "You didn't do the dishes yet. They're still in the sink."

"I'll do them when I get back," Tara challenged.

"No, you won't, you'll do them now," my stepfather's voice rose to the point of eruption.

Tara's reply held the note of sass, which reached our stepfather's ear. "Whatever, geez," she replied. Our stepfather's face turned red with rage, and his stance took on the look of a bear ready for battle. Instead of responding, he lumbered toward her, and Tara knew what was coming next.

"Go ahead, hit me," my sister responded in defiance as she stood beside Jackie who wore a look of utter disbelief. From the safe distance of space, I watched the man who ruled our household with an iron fist drop his hand in surprise and never raise it toward my sister, or me, again. His voice, though, continued to make us cower well into our adult years.

When we were young, Tara and I chose to defy our stepfather most often when he was not around to find out. Occasionally, if he and my mother were not home, we'd turn the knob of the TV and watch "General Hospital" with furtive looks out the window every time we heard a sound beyond the screen. At friends' houses, and when we were in Oregon, we gleefully absorbed our monthly allowance of TV in one sitting, and didn't care that none of it was PBS.

At other times, it was more difficult for me to leave our household rules behind. One day, when I was about ten-years-old and over at Margot's, I left the door open while I was going to the bathroom. Margot, who didn't seem to care, came in and started chatting with me while perched on the edge of the tub. After I finished peeing, then wiped, she gave me a funny look.

"What are you doing?"

I looked from my now empty hand, to the trash can, and my face started to burn.

"Oops," I said. "I guess I wasn't paying attention."

At home, after he had installed the indoor toilet, my stepfather made the rule that all used tissue not soiled with feces must be placed in the trash can. "It clogs the septic," he told me, Tara and our mother. "And, don't flush unless you go poop."

Although I sometimes forgot, like that day at Margot's house, I tried my best to pretend that I led a normal life. If my friends happened to see the marijuana tucked away amid the ferns behind our outhouse, I dutifully told them they were tomato plants, and then hurried them along. I got in the habit of making sure I flushed the toilet (with tissue) at other people's houses, and I told my friends that my stepfather was not to be called my stepfather, but my dad.

There were some things I could not hide, like the food I brought for lunch in grade school when we were still vegetarians. In the cafeteria I would look around the table and wistfully watch my friends with their saran-wrapped sandwiches made of bread that looked like clouds, all soft, white and full of air, cushioning pink baloney and squares of orange cheese. Oh, how I wanted to sink my teeth into those sandwiches!

One day, while I sat with my friends at the cafeteria table, one of them pointed at my sandwich, while wrinkling her nose. "What are those?" she asked. Her fingers threatened to touch the little green shoots that looked like they were struggling to grow out of their bed of brown, seedy bread.

"Sprouts," I mumbled.

"Sprouts? What are sprouts?!"

With the question, my face grew hot, as though I was suddenly standing, against my will, too close to an open fire.

"I don't know," I whispered looking down at my lunch, wishing by some grace of the universe that it would disappear. "They're kind-of like lettuce, only smaller."

"Well they look like grass. What are you, a cow?"

The fire in my face flamed, while my eyes watered to quench it. My stomach, in turn, had closed to the prospect of taking another bite.

I didn't throw my sandwich away. I never did. Instead I wrapped the nibbled remains back into their waxed paper package, and handed them shamefully to my mother at the end of the day. "Alethea," she asked me, shaking her head. "Why didn't you eat more of your lunch?"

My victims

churn with guilt

I run
an invisible
chase with
time

awkwardly touching
the feral
twist of

thought

I stumble over
betrayal

One spring day, when I was in the first grade, I made my first and only trip to the principal's office. My victim was Timmy, a chubby boy with light blond hair and blue eyes hidden behind thick glasses. Timmy didn't have any friends, and that day on the playground he sat, as usual, by himself on a bench while the rest of the school played around him.

I began recess on the swing-set with my best-friend of the day, Stacy. As we soared over the ground, we giggled and made faces of disgust, pointing our fingers at Timmy, who studied the brown dirt beside his feet.

When we grew bored and hopped off the swings, Stacy whispered into my ear, "I dare you to go over to Timmy and tell him he's fat."

I hesitated, "Only if you go with me."

Together Stacy and I ran past Timmy, crying out in nervous giggles, "Timmy, you're fat! Timmy, why are you so fat?"

Timmy never lifted his gaze from the ground, but the teacher on playground duty caught our words as they skipped through the air.

"Alethea and Stacy," she called after us, "Please come with me to the principal's office."

While I sat with Stacy on the bench outside the closed door of the office, my stomach churned with guilt and fear. Tears spilled from the corners of my eyes as I contemplated the reprimand that awaited us. All of my previous punishments at school had been for talking in class and passing notes. I felt awful for myself, and deep within my belly, I felt awful for Timmy, who was more like me than I wanted to admit.

I never teased Timmy again, instead I mostly watched, with the mixed pang of relief and guilt, when a child who wasn't me suffered the ridicule of being different. I couldn't, though, resist tormenting Sally.

No one really liked Sally, or wanted to be around her. Sally wore glasses, and without them her eyes crossed. Her hair hung in stringy strands down her back, and most days Sally looked like she needed a bath.

When we played tag, Sally was the one with cooties, and my friends and I would run away whenever she came near. If she touched us, we would invent an invisible shower under the hemlock trees, and stand there until we were cleansed of her germs. The boys, in turn, loved to chase Sally with their homemade spitball guns constructed out of lunchroom straws. They shot their ammunition, saliva soaked wads of paper, with their breath, hoping to land the dripping pulp on the skin, or even better, the glasses of Sally.

"Splat."

"Got her," the victorious boy would yell.

My friends and I giggled nervously, while we peered at Sally and the goo that covered the glass over her eye in dripping humiliation. We stared and waited for Sally to wipe away the trail of slime as it slid down the side of her cheek. Sally, in turn, never cried. Instead, she held tight her emotions like a seasoned soldier.

At school I made a point of shunning Sally, while doing my best to fit in. I acted like the other girls in my class I wanted to be like, the girls whose lives seemed on the surface, like Margot's, almost perfect.

I met Ann one sunny morning in the fourth grade while Margot and I were engaged in a game of double-dutch on the playground with two other girls. It was impossible not to notice Ann strolling through the parking lot with the principal as though she already belonged.

Walking our way was a girl we had never seen before, proudly sporting pink capris tied in bows below her knees and a matching vest. The outfit, I thought, was wonderful, but even better was the hat she wore on her head. This too matched, with its thick pink bow wrapped above a wide straw brim. No one in the fourth grade had a hat like that. How bold she was, I thought, as I watched her approach with an easy smile spread across her freckled face. Surely, she must have come from a bigger, more impressive town than ours.

She had, as she generously shared that first day on the playground. Like Margot, Ann was not shy. She answered with pleasure all of our questions about her past and present life, happy already to be the center of our attention. I envied Ann's confidence, as I often envied Margot's.

For the first few weeks after her arrival, everyone wanted to be Ann's best friend, including Margot and me. Margot had the advantage of having Ann in her classroom, but I did a good job of making up for lost time on the playground, in the cafeteria, and during weekend sleepovers.

There were other times that I spent with just Margot. Days when she and I were best-friends. Like the day in the fifth grade when Margot came up with the idea to go roller skating with two boys from our class. I remember my hesitation before I agreed to Margot's plan. Margot's parents were recently divorced, and she had only to deceive her mother. I had to evade suspicion from both my mother and stepfather. I hated lying and tried to avoid it at all costs. I was never any good at it, and even a small white lie would fill me with a guilt that I was breaking that vow of "truth" I had made at birth. More than that, though, I worried my parents would find out.

Instead of blatantly lying, I told my mother only the information I wanted her to know: that Margot and I wanted to go roller skating in Concord. As I recall, my mother hesitated before she agreed, suspecting already that I was leaving something out. My mother didn't trusted Margot, and I wasn't much of a liar.

Margot invited the two boys she wanted to come along, both of whom happened to like her. She knew I liked the boy with blond hair and blue eyes, and she was, at the time, more interested in his friend.

It was, for me, a miserable day. While Margot glided around the rink hand-in-hand with her boyfriend, the blue-eyed boy and I shuffled awkwardly, without touching, across the gray concrete. When it was time to meet my mother outside the building, Margot and her chosen boy had disappeared into a dark corner. After I found the hiding couple, Margot asked the boys to accompany us outside.

"But, my mother will see them," I protested.

"Oh come on Alethea," she said, "Just tell her we didn't know they would be here."

My mother kept silent until after we dropped Margot off at her house. As we pulled out of the driveway, she turned to me.

"Why didn't you tell me you were meeting boys?" she asked.

I couldn't look at my mother's face, so I focused my eyes on hands that had grown cold upon my lap.

"Because I knew you wouldn't let me go. It was Margot's idea. Both of the boys like her," I added. "I don't even have a boyfriend."

The following year, Margot, Ann, and I, along with fourteen other children, graduated from the small elementary school in Canterbury, NH. It should have been a happy occasion, and it was, for the most part. Earlier in the day, my stepfather and I went to a lumber mill in town where he had heard there was a litter of feral kittens. After much running around, we managed to catch a fluffy white male with two smears of gray grease above his eyes. I named him Huey, and immediately fell in love. He was all mine — the best graduation gift I received.

114

For the graduation ceremony I wore a blue-and-white dress my mother made for me. She twisted my shoulder-length hair into a French braid with sprigs of lavender from her garden tucked into the folds. I felt pretty and decidedly older as I sat with my class of seventeen and thought about moving beyond our small town. For me, junior high in the neighboring town of Belmont held the promise of new girlfriends, and the more thrilling possibility of boyfriends.

As I sat listening to Margot give the valedictory address on that June evening, I realized how much I envied her. The Math Award, a blue and white certificate I had received that evening, did not equal Margot's place on the podium. Even though Margot's parents were now divorced and her mother seemed to have a new boyfriend each week, which was a hot subject for town gossip, I still thought Margot had the better life.

That evening, alone in the bedroom I shared with Tara, I opened up the white cover of the graduation program and read through the words typed in black ink. It was only one sheet of folded paper, and it didn't take me long to get through the list of seventeen alphabetized names. I found my name in the middle under "F" and felt the unavoidable rise of heat. "Fischer, Aletha Eamon." I read the three words used to define me, barely noticing the omission of the "e" from my first name. It was the middle name that brought the burn of shame. Eamon. I had held this part of me inside for more than twelve years. Eamon. A name I thought no one knew outside of my family. When my friends shared their pretty middle names, I never shared mine. Now, alone in my room, I felt naked and utterly exposed. I had no way to cover-up what everyone had already seen.

As I stared hard at the paper in my hand, I heard my mother's voice speak through the neurons of my brain. "It was Dave's idea. He wanted you to be a boy." *Why,* I thought desperately as tears filled the corners of my eyes, *didn't you care enough to give me another name? A pretty girl's name? A name I wouldn't want to hide?*

I didn't ask my mother how my middle name had found its place on the program. Instead, I folded the paper back together and buried it in a box in my closet with the hope that my classmates had not noticed what had appeared in black ink.

For a while I forgot about the name that was no longer a secret. No one said anything to me about it, and Ann and I happily made preparations to head off to over-night camp together on Lake Winnipesaukee. One day, while Ann and I spoke on the phone, comparing what we were packing for camp, Ann confided that her mother had given her a package of sanitary napkins to take with her. Just in case. I immediately worried Ann would start her period before me, even though I was older by nearly eight months. I still had only a hint of breasts, and my mother hadn't offered to buy me a box of pads, just in case.

A few months later, Margot showed me her own package of sanitary napkins, tucked neatly behind the pink curtain below her bathroom sink. This, of course, only added to my paranoia that another friend would start menstruating before me. Margot was also eight months younger than me. So I called Ann, trying to hide my anxiety while I laughed, "As if she'll need those for a while!"

As friends do, Ann later called Margot, who confronted me about my comment. Instead of lying, I tried to downplay my words. "I just thought it was weird that your mom bought you pads already," I stumbled over my excuse.

***

After I returned from camp with Ann, I had my last visit with my father. I didn't know when I boarded the plane with my sister that

116

our summers in Oregon were coming to an end. I didn't know when I said good-bye to Grammie on the green grass of her front lawn, it would be the last time I felt her embrace.

That July, Tara and I spent our last night on the top of Mt. Scott. We took our final dives into the blue chlorine waters of my grandparents' pool and happily dried our skin on their sun-baked deck while consuming cans of pop, chips, and my grandmother's kiln-dried Granny Smith apples. We had no idea that nine years would pass before we saw Oregon and most of our birth relatives again.

Instead, the summer of 1986 played out much the same as the previous four had. Tara and I drove to the seacoast with our father and went on hikes through the Oregon forests. My father had down-sized to a gray Subaru Brat with two bucket seats in the front, and a small truck-like bed in the back. Even today he remembers, with a chuckle, our irritation at having to squish our too-large bodies to-gether in one awkward row meant for two people.

Although our stepfather had stopped smoking marijuana, our fa-ther would still make detours during our drives together to purchase a bag of its dried leaves, then roll them into reefers after Tara and I went to bed. Often, at night, we would catch the sweet smell of its dried leaves as they smoldered and billowed their smoke through the night air and into our loft bedroom. In an effort to clear the air, we would place a fan in the window, facing outward. Instead of con-fronting our father, we pretended we didn't know what he was do-ing, that it is, until we got back home and told our mother and step-father.

When we flew home that summer, our mother, as she had grown accustomed to, remarked about our sullenness, attributing it to the mind-games of her mother and the sub-par parenting skills of her ex-husband. She was right in some respects. Traveling to Ore-

117

gon each summer did mess with our minds. The moments of fun Tara and I experienced with our relatives were always tainted by guilt, along with the notion that pleasure equaled betrayal of the person we loved most. Our mother.

In my memory, the four of us were sitting at the kitchen table eating dinner the day my mother and stepfather told us of their plan to end our visits to Oregon. "Just think, you won't have to see Dave anymore or sleep in that shed of his," my mother convinced us. "I can't believe he smokes pot in front of you girls and is still mooching off his mother."

My mother paused, glancing over at our stepfather for his approval and support before she continued, "And you won't have to put up with my nosey mother asking you girls questions all the time and trying to make you feel guilty. She's always messing up your minds. You girls don't even like going out there. You're never happy when you return. It gets worse every year and you always come home all screwed up."

I lacked the power to deny my mother's words, especially in the presence of my stepfather. At home, it was almost impossible for me to view my relatives in Oregon, especially my father, as family, let alone family who really loved us. Inside the walls of my heart, I struggled with love. I wanted to believe my mother's words, if only to please her, but I also wanted to tell her that she was wrong. That in Oregon I sometimes experienced moments of pure joy, moments when I felt like I was part of two large, extended families filled with cousins, laughter and fun. When I looked over at my sister, I read my thoughts in her face, which turned away from my mother's words to the untouched food on her plate. I felt the brief impulse of protest as I held back the words that fired through the synapses of my brain, *No. I'm not sure.*

Weeks later, I sat in a small brown lobby waiting to be called inside a room where a lawyer sat at a desk piled with papers. My mind churned with words that were not my own. I saw my father's resigned face the day we sat together on the quilt under the pines and he reluctantly relinquished the title of "dad." In a few moments I would, with my sister, cut the tenuous hold he held on his daughters. I felt the turmoil of his loss under my mother's words, and buried beneath it, I felt my own.

As part of the protocol to determine if we should in fact stop going out to see our father, the lawyer asked my sister and me to a draw picture. Any picture. It didn't matter, only we knew it did. Tara recalls being frustrated by this request, because, as she told me, she didn't know what to draw. Eventually her hand formed the arc of a rainbow, using the box of crayons she had been given, because, she would later tell me, she liked rainbows. I think perhaps I drew a rainbow too, but I can't say for sure. I can see an uneven arc spread in waxy hues across a manila sky, and the drip of rain around it that later made my mother and stepfather upset with me.

When it was time for words, they came in the form of those rehearsed days previous at the dinner table and during the car ride over. I was nervous when I said them across the wooden desk, wondering if the man on the other side would believe me, wondering if I believed me. "No," I said. "I don't want to see him anymore."

When I was fourteen

i took

the backseat, tightly belted into
anxiety
I
wrapped misery

beside me
and
took her
hand

The first year of junior high proved to be everything I had hoped for and more. After being over-looked by the boys from my hometown throughout most of elementary school, I was suddenly feeling both pretty and popular. A week rarely passed without a boy asking me to be his girlfriend, and I was invited to all the parties that mattered. As I immersed myself into this new, wonderful experience called junior high, Margot and Ann became less of a focus in my life. They, in turn, remained close.

The three of us were still friends though, and Margot was often the conduit between me and the boys who became my boyfriends. She loved being in charge of my romances. Margot arranged the venue for my first French kiss, waiting with Ann in a silent room next door, while a boy I only sort-of liked stuck his tongue inside my mouth in the dark closet of the band room. Throughout the seventh grade, Margot happily played cupid for me and the boys I thought were cute, but not even Margot knew what to do with Jason. Jason was the first boy to vie for my affection in the seventh grade. We were in the same homeroom, and even though he sat two rows behind me, each morning I could feel the flames of his blue eyes burning the nape of my neck. I must confess, I loved their heat.

Each time Jason asked me out I turned him down, finding it incredibly satisfying that his affections never waned. I was smart enough to know Jason was trouble. Aside from his enthusiasm for sports, Jason was a classic under-achiever. He spent the majority of his time goofing-off in class and harassing the pretty girls. I was, in contrast, an over-achiever. I made the honor-roll, joined the math and trivia teams, and was a three sport athlete who often won awards. Aside from talking too much in class, I was a model student.

Instead of accepting Jason's pleas to be his girlfriend, I chose other boys, including Mark. Mark was a tall handsome eighth grader, who happened to be the only boy to ever dump me, which he did

121

off and on for the next two years. Whenever he decided he liked me again, I'd happily take him back. It was Mark who brought me to the junior high prom.

That evening, my sister and I waited together for his arrival, watching from the window at the top of the stairs outside our bedroom. When my date stepped out of the car looking nervous in his tan jacket, pink tie, and brown hair parted into commas on the sides of his forehead, Tara began to giggle.

I wanted to kick her for laughing. I thought Mark looked perfect, too perfect, perhaps, for me in my homemade pink satin dress and cheap black flats topped with large, hand-sewn bows. I had finally started my period, and thought about the pad tucked inside my underwear, hoping I would make it safely through the night without a stain.

As soon as Mark stepped out of his family's station wagon with his mother and his sister, I worried that my mother would welcome them inside our funky, still unfinished home. Like a proper host, she did. While I watched Mark's mother scan the items in our combination living room, dining room and kitchen, I wanted to sink into the brick of the floor. I was sure our entire downstairs was the size of Mark's living room alone, and I was certain his mother was inwardly judging our funky handmade couch with its back of wooden slats, the bumpy discolored brick floor, and our tiny living space. I couldn't wait to leave.

During the twenty minute ride to the prom, Mark's mother chatted with us from the driver's seat, but I was too nervous to muster more than one word answers. I couldn't stop thinking about my house and comparing it to the home I imagined was Mark's. In the privacy of my mind, I built his house in two large stories, and painted its wooden siding a sage green. I gave it a white wrap-around porch that overlooked a lake. Downstairs, I partitioned the rooms into four separate squares, and added a large rectangular bathroom. Upstairs, I designed four spacious bedrooms, one for each child, along with two additional bathrooms. When I was finished, Mark's house looked grand and proud sitting beside the water with nothing to hide.

The prom, itself, was largely uneventful, and by the beginning of the next school year Mark had moved on to high school and other girls. The beginning of eighth grade, for me, was a lot like seventh grade. Jason was still sitting behind me in homeroom, trying to get me to go out with him. Margot and Ann, who were again sharing a homeroom and the same sports, were closer than ever, but I pretended not to notice. That is, until they started dating Matt and Brian.

Matt and Brian were also best friends, but they were in the tenth grade. The two boys were not very popular among their peers, but the fact that they were in high school was all that really mattered to me and my classmates. Within a few weeks, Margot and Ann were proudly displaying their boyfriends' class rings on their thumbs, and had won the envy of the eighth grade girls. We coveted their rings so much that some of us decided we also had to date boys from the tenth grade.

Before I started dating a sophomore, I danced with Margot's boyfriend. Margot was at her father's house for the weekend, but that didn't dissuade Brian from going to the dance without her. I didn't have a boyfriend, so I went with my best friend Ellen who was more interested in cross-country running than in boys. Ellen looked inconspicuous in her jeans and t-shirt, but I was dressed to be noticed. My legs, shaved from the knees down, were bare under a jean miniskirt and I had on my favorite royal blue, three-quarter-sleeved blouse that matched the color of my eyes. I knew I looked good.

The first time Margot's boyfriend asked me to dance I hesitated.

"Oh, come on. It's no big deal. It's just a dance," he told me with a smile that should have made me turn away.

Instead, I let Brian's arms nestle into the curve of my back while the lyrics of Heart lured our bodies together. When the music slowed a second time, and Margot's boyfriend began making his way across the dance floor, I noticed Ann's face framed in the shadows.

"You want to dance?" Brian asked again as though he had already forgotten the girl spending the weekend at her father's.

"I'm not sure that's a good idea," I said, nervously looking around for Ann.

The arms that wrapped me had grown bolder, and by the middle of the song their hands were resting on the rise of my butt.

"You look pretty tonight," Brian whispered in my ear. Ann, I saw, was watching us like a museum security guard while she danced in the arms of her boyfriend.

A third time he returned. It seemed this boy had no guilt, and in the moment after he asked me for another dance, I flirted with power. What if, I wondered, I gave him one more dance? If I let his skin feel mine through the shield of denim, would he go back to her? I didn't want Margot's boyfriend, though. In my eyes he was more annoying than cute, even in the muted light of the cafeteria. Besides, I was not the kind of girl who would deliberately steal something that didn't belong to me.

The Monday after the dance, I saw Margot with Brian, walking closely beside Ann and Matt. I knew I was in trouble. During the course of the day, whenever I crossed their path, Margot and Ann would sneer, whisper and look away. By lunchtime I was sure the whispers that followed their gaze were directed at me. I knew Ann had told Margot about the dance, and in the mix of her words I had become the one to blame.

On Tuesday, I opened my locker to find magazine cutouts of Rob Lowe and Tom Cruise defaced with black marker bearing the words "Cunt" and "Bitch." A quick rise of red spread across my features as I listened to my locker-mate, Jane, catch her breath behind me. When I turned to look at her, Jane merely shook her head, gathered her books, and walked on down the hallway. I was crushed. This was a girl I considered my friend, a girl I had met in seventh grade and who had come over to my house for a sleepover. Jane had slept in my bed while I slept on the bottom bunk that used to be my sister's.

The next night, after Jane went home, I had pulled down the covers and crawled in between the sheets. My bare skin recoiled when it met the cool sensation of moisture. It could only be urine, I realized. Annoyed and embarrassed for her, I changed the bedding, but never mentioned Jane's accident to anyone at school.

Now, standing alone by our locker, I felt utterly betrayed and alone. I wanted to vanish into the obscurity of air. Instead, I followed my classmates to science class. The snickers started in the front row, and followed the attendance cards to the back of the room where I was seated. The red that had not left my face was now searing. On the index card with my name, the word "smells" appeared in blue ink.

Faces now turned my way whenever I passed a group of students in the hallway. Eating lunch under the florescent glare of the cafeteria lights became nearly impossible. Through the steady drone of voices I was sure I could hear the whisper of my name. Laughter inevitably followed.

I hated going to school. Each morning I woke to the fear of what Margot and Ann might have in store for me that day. I was paranoid about rumors I knew where circulating about me. My long history with Margot had convinced me of her gift for fabrication and

125

exaggeration. No one cared to share what they were saying about me, and I was too ashamed to ask. The realization that most boys were no longer asking me out, and the popular girls were now shunning my presence, was really all I needed to know.

It didn't take long for Brian and Matt to join in my humiliation. Margot and Ann, it became evident, had also read their programs after sixth grade graduation.

"Hey, Eamon! *Eamon!*" the middle name my father gave the girl he wanted to be a boy, chased me down the hallway in the voices of Matt and Brian. I felt mortified and shamed. Margot and Ann, I realized, were sparing no measure of embarrassment to ruin my life.

One day, I passed Margot and Ann on my way to math class. "Look, she's wearing a skirt again," they whispered loudly to the students around them. "That means she's having her period." Somehow I made through class and the rest of the day, but later, when I got home, I asked my mother if I could start wearing tampons.

Another day, I stepped off the school bus, opened the metal door of our mailbox, and pulled out its contents. On the top of the envelopes addressed to my parents, there was a small rectangular package with my name on it. A spark of excitement traveled through my chest as I wondered about this unexpected surprise.

Alone in my bedroom, I tore through the brown paper to reveal an envelope on top of a white box. On the white surface I read the words, *Gentle Glide,* in pink italics. A flush of red filled my face as I opened the flap at the top of the container and removed one of the six cylinders encased in pearly white paper. The wrapper tore easily with the pull of my fingers, revealing a pink plastic tube. The tampons were much nicer than the blunt-edged cardboard ones I'd just started to use.

It must be a promotional mailing, I thought, but my hands shook while I opened the letter that I would never be able to finish.

126

The first words were nice. In fact they were so nice, they mocked me as I read answers to questions I had never asked. The author of the letter, a representative of the tampon company, thanked me for inquiring about their products, while politely explaining that it was perfectly safe to wear tampons overnight, for up to seven hours, and that yes, masturbation with a tampon was normal and okay. The white paper trembled with the shake of my hands, and its black words blurred with the water now filling my eyes.

Is this what they were now telling people, I wondered, that I liked to masturbate with tampons? In a flash of anger, I imagined folding the letter back into an envelope with a simple note: Here are the answers to the questions you were wondering about. I considered adding the word Slut at the end before I licked it sealed without a signature. In the darkness of night, I thought, I'd deliver the letter to Margot's mailbox.

Instead, I gathered the contents of my "gift" and presented it to my mother, who was melting lead onto colored glass in her studio. She placed the hot iron on its stand and looked into my burning face. My mother looked angry and tired as she read through the contents of the letter.

"Those little bitches," she said after she finished.

Although I had chosen to share only a fraction of the humiliation I had endured during the past year with my mother, it was enough for her to know that my life at school had been ruined by my two former friends. I was turning into a moody and despondent teenager, spending as much time as possible inside my bedroom. That day would be the first and only time in my memory that my mother would take action to defend me.

Standing beside her, I watched my mother pick up the phone and dial Margot's number. I waited with my breath held inside my trembling chest for the ring of her call to be answered. While my mother spoke with Margot's mother, I mentally filled in the words I imagined were coming through the speaker of the phone. There was a pause, too short, while Margot's mother abandoned her connection to find her daughter.

"Okay," I heard my mother's resigned reply before she hung up the phone. In that moment I knew I had lost again. Margot, I discovered, decided it wasn't worth the effort to lie about what she had done.

"Well, at least she admitted it," my mother told me as she dialed Ann's number.

Ann's mother took the stance of defensive denial, just like her daughter, who had yet to learn that her best-friend had already confessed. Ann pleaded innocence, and her mother accepted her plea before hanging up the phone.

"Well, I did what I could, Alethea," my mother told me, "Hopefully they'll stop harassing you now."

I waited for the apology from Margot and Ann I never got. I waited for my life to go back to the way it was before the dance. Instead, I suffered the fate of silence. Margot and Ann stopped openly shaming me, but continued to treat me as though I was an Untouchable, as did most of our peers. I had gone from the top to the bottom of the social castes of junior high in less than a year, and I couldn't figure out how to climb my way back up. Although their boyfriends no longer shouted "Eamon" down the hallways when I passed, the popular students were still shunning me. When I dared to look at Margot and Ann, their faces were smug and cruel.

I still couldn't walk down the halls at school without worrying that every whispered word was about me. I couldn't answer questions in class or converse with a group of people without blood rushing to cover my face in shame. Even today if I let my mind wonder too much about another person's thoughts, I can't hold a conversation without the familiar mask of red.

The day Margot and Ann's focus turned on another girl, I felt my paranoia slightly abate. We were now in the tenth grade, the three of us learning archery with our peers on the school grounds during gym class. While taking aim, I heard the loud whispers of Margot's and Ann's voices, and instinctively turned from my focus on the bull's eye to see if their gazes were directed my way. I shot my arrow with a surge of relief. The two girls, I discovered, were concentrating on Alice, and in particular her ass. It was the only flaw they could find on her, and that day Alice's behind was accentuated by tight white pants.

When it was Alice's turn to try her hand shooting at the large white circle, Ann and Margot started snickering again among their huddle of friends. Boys included.

"Look at her ass," one of them said. "It could be the target."

Everyone laughed. The boys, even though they all, no doubt, harbored secret crushes on Alice, as she was beautiful, joined in. While I watched, I felt the pang of pleasure that it wasn't just me.

I learned

to downshift, instead of break
I learned

to coast
in the way
of opposition
I feared the
quick
rise of rage
enough to question

my
Truth

My father made his last trip to New Hampshire to visit us when Tara was learning how to drive. Usually it was my stepfather who took my sister out for driving lessons, but I can recall a day during his visit when my father invited Tara to take the wheel of his rental car.

It was the first time he had a car with a backseat, and I sat tightly belted into my anxiety, while my sister drove us to our destination, our old hometown of Henniker. That day we had lunch at Daniel's Restaurant by the Contookook River and wandered around the downtown. My father tried to carry on a conversation about how things had changed in New Hampshire over the years, but my sister and I were too wrapped in our adolescent angst to care about his words.

Tara drove us partway home to Canterbury. I imagine she must have been nervous behind the wheel with our father beside her and me in the backseat, perhaps more nervous than she was when she would drive with our stepfather. Or, maybe Tara felt a surge of power; of control over this man who nervously tried to correct her mistakes. After all, it was her hand, along with mine, who had signed the papers that took away his right to see us each summer. Even with my sister in the driver's seat, our ride together felt a lot like our drives in Oregon had. It felt awkward and long, as did the brief time we spent together that week.

We took a detour through Concord before we drove home. The stop had been prearranged with our mother, but our father was unaware of our plan.

"Um, do you mind if we stop at a store on Main Street?" Tara asked him.

When Tara pulled up in front of the sporting goods store, our father looked puzzled, but followed us inside. "Tell him you need new

131

ski equipment," my mother had instructed us. "It's the least he can do. He never buys you girls anything."

While Tara and I nervously sorted through the racks of new skis, we glanced anxiously at our father. Although he looked confused, he didn't deter us once he figured out why we were there. Instead, he mumbled about the unanticipated expense, while trying his best to play the part of an indulgent father. It was the first time we had asked him for anything.

With the help of a sales clerk, Tara and I chose twin sets of white alpine skis with fluorescent lettering, and matching boots. The poles were the only thing that didn't look the same. The ski sets, at least, were on sale, but while I watched with buried guilt, my father write the check, I could see by his dazed expression that it would take him a long time to recover from this unanticipated expense.

***

I too learned to drive under the guidance of my stepfather. Never, in my memory, did he lose his temper when I was behind the wheel, not even the time I nearly ruined the engine of my mother's new Honda Accord by stepping on the gas while trying to downshift, instead of the break, causing the car to skid and holler down the snowy slope of our driveway.

I drove my stepfather's truck only on occasion, usually through town, and primarily on weekends to help him bring our trash to the dump just over a mile from our house. That is, until one fateful summer day before I turned seventeen.

The four of us where on our way to the seacoast to attend a gathering of families from town at a neighbor's summer home. Before we left, my stepfather announced that I was going to drive his pick-up, while the rest of my family led the way in my mother's

Honda. Driving the truck, especially alone, filled me with dread, but I knew I couldn't refuse. Any protest I made would be met with my stepfather's opposition — and possibly his anger. Even at sixteen, I feared the consequences that might arise from disobeying his orders. The thought of telling him I didn't want to drive his truck, that I wasn't comfortable with it, was not an option I felt I could voice. I feared his rage more than I did the drive ahead. My throat bore the memory of his hand clenching my words when I dared to defy his will.

Even though I wanted desperately to ride in the car with my mother and sister, I climbed onto the hot brown vinyl of his truck. I reached under my legs for the lever to move the seat forward until my feet touched the pedals. My internal temperature was already rising faster than the heat from the sun. I felt wholly inadequate to be driving a beast of a vehicle on roads and highways I had never driven down before. Cursing my stepfather under my breath, I turned the key, shifted the lever down to D, and waited for him to pull ahead so I could follow my family's sedan.

The drive through Canterbury was bumpy and uneventful, but as we turned onto the less familiar backroads of Chichester, my unease began to grow. Through the dust of the road I gripped the steering wheel and concentrated on the small blue car ahead. At the intersection to turn onto coastal Rt. 4, I watched my family's car pull through the two lanes of traffic, and, worried about losing sight of it, I pulled out too.

The first vehicle to veer off the road in an attempt to miss me was a Jeep traveling in the opposite direction. With my heart pumping adrenaline, I saw four people tip dangerously out of its open sides. In the rearview mirror I watched the Jeep skid to a stop in a path of rubber on the road where I had begun my turn. I could hear the cursing shouts of its occupants, and filled with fear and guilt, I

133

pushed the gas petal once again to avoid the screech of the cars behind me. Miraculously, no one was harmed by my carelessness.

Although my heart was in my throat, I didn't stop after this
near-accident because neither had my stepfather. In fact, he was nowhere in sight. So I drove on, peering anxiously ahead for a glimpse
of our blue Honda, which I eventually located, pulled over about a
half-mile up the road. I had hoped that after nearly killing myself
and at least eight other people, I would now be removed from the
driver's seat. I slowed down, ready to pull off the road, but my stepfather, upon seeing his truck, inched the Honda onto the lane ahead
of me. I was left with no choice but to follow.

The ensuing forty miles to Portsmouth proved uneventful, aside
from the churning of my body and emotions. When we reached the
city, we pulled off the highway, and my stepfather began traversing
the maze-like cobbled side streets with me following dutifully behind.

"Is he trying to kill me?!" I swore out loud, as I tried to navigate
the increasingly narrow roads with his too-wide truck.

Eventually, I had to make a choice. It was either the car parked
on my right, or the mailbox, jutting into the road on my left. I chose
the mailbox, cringing while I watched the driver's side mirror fold
inward toward my door. Again, we did not stop, and I finished the
rest of the trip with one mirror down.

On this day, as it often does, bad luck came in threes. Pulling
onto the residential road near our destination, I looked around for a
place to park. Vehicles already lined the roadside for the party, and I
could see groups of people mingling with plates of food and drinks
in their hands. My stepfather, ahead of me, had found a gap, and
seamlessly navigated the Honda into a space between two cars.
There were no empty spots that could fit the truck, so I turned in an
effort to back up. My fender met resistance in the form of a granite

light post at the end of the host's driveway, loosening the stone pillar from the soil and sending it with a horrifying thud to the ground.

The last thing I wanted to do was exit the truck, but it was time to face my stepfather, the host whose post I had toppled, and the other guests I knew from Canterbury, who, I was certain, had all witnessed the spectacle and were now getting a nice chuckle out of it. Ann and her family included.

My stepfather was waiting for me when I emerged from his truck, and together we went to find the host. Since I had caused the accident, I knew my stepfather expected me to do the speaking. Stumbling through my words, with my stepfather beside me, I apologized to our neighbor, who looked from the fallen post to my red face.

"It's okay," he said, "Don't worry about it. I just had it put in the other day and they needed to come back anyway to secure it into the ground." All I could think about, at that moment while I mumbled my gratitude, was how much I hated my stepfather.

***

I had begun to date boys that were a lot like my stepfather. After Margot and Ann turned against me, I, without consciously realizing it, chose to go out with boys who tried to control me. The first boy, Steve, was a muscular sixteen-year-old, who was in the tenth grade when I was in the eighth. I agreed to go out with Steve to be like Margot, Ann and the other girls who were also dating high school boys. It was, I hoped, a way to become cool again. A way to recover some of my self-esteem.

Steve was really in love with my sister, and as much as I tried to, I didn't really like him all that much. The best thing about dating Steve was that I got to wear his class ring, which bore a large, fake diamond in the middle of its chunky silver band. Steve wanted more than kisses from me, and after I let him guide my hand to his large erection one day while we watched TV under a blanket in his living room, I knew I was in over my head. The romance was short-lived.

Although there were still a few boys in my school who thought they were in love with me, I wasn't attracted to the nice guys. Instead, two years after I broke up with Steve, I said "yes" to Jason. To my sixteen-year-old mind, he was my best option. I should have known what I was getting into. In the seventh grade I had heard rumors that Jason and a well-developed girl in our class had engaged in sexual acts while they were still in grade school. Even though I had known since the seventh grade that Jason was trouble, that didn't stop me from going out with him.

It was a regrettable three months, but the truth is during those weeks I fell for Jason. In my vulnerability, he won me over with his doting and smothering charm. He called my house at least once a night, and wrote me notes on scraps of paper passed up the rows in biology class. "You're beautiful." "I love you." He filled the white space in blue ink before he folded the paper and placed my name on the top. Jason, in his suffocating manner, made me feel pretty and special again.

While I was going out with Jason, he came over to my house only once. During the visit, my parents decided to drive the mile up the road to the center store to look for a movie to watch later in the evening. They left the two of us alone for the fifteen minutes it took them to make the round trip. While my parents were gone, we made out in my bedroom, fully clothed, but that wasn't a good enough story for Jason to share with his buddies on Monday.

A few days later, I was eating lunch with Jason and a group of his friends.

"Hey red-winger!" A boy from the ninth grade called over to me, and then burst into laughter while his buddies slapped him on the back.

I had no idea what he meant, but I knew by the way Jason was blushing and his friends were laughing, that it couldn't be good.

"What are they talking about?" I whispered to Jason as my face reddened.

"Oh, nothing. They're just being dorks. Ignore them," he replied.

I was beginning to distrust Jason, but I also thought I loved him. Days later, a friend of mine was kind enough to fill me in on the rumors circulating about me. I learned that Jason had woven a fantastic story about having sex with me on my bed while my parents were at the center store. Why he felt the need to add the embellishment that I was having my period, I will never understand.

When I confronted Jason about the rumor, his denial broke my heart.

"I don't know what you're talking about. I never told anyone we had sex," he said. As much as I wanted to believe him, I knew Jason was lying.

After I broke up with him, Jason followed me around the school begging me to take him back. He didn't seem to care who was watching his groveling, and I found his behavior more embarrassing than flattering.

Jason had persistence, and he wasn't easy to convince that it was over between us. One day, he followed me to my locker and barricaded me with the walls of his arms while I attempted to gather my books into my backpack. "Don't break up with me," he pleaded, lowering his arms down the metal surface of the locker as I tried to duck under them.

"Leave me alone," I said, looking around for support, while a part of me thrilled at his devotion.

The hallway was emptying out, but at least we were not alone. Jason, finally catching on, followed my glances and lowered his arms.

As the week wore on, Jason continued to follow me around the school begging me to take him back. In the evenings, he called my house.

He was relentless, and also angry. One afternoon, as my sister and I approached our car after ski practice, I heard her exclaim, "What the hell happened to our license plate?!"

The plate once bolted to the back of our white 1977 Chevy Malibu was gone. We searched the snowbanks, Tara cursing Jason under her breath, while my heart raced.

"Why the hell did you ever go out with that jerk?" Tara asked during the ride home.

The license plate hadn't been found, but we both knew whose prints were on it.

My stepfather, angered by the loss of the plate, intervened, calling Jason's house later that night. As I listened to my stepfather's side of the conversation, I could tell Jason was denying the charge we had placed against him. The power of my stepfather's voice grew until it filled the room, and I knew things were not going the way he wanted them to.

The next day someone found our license plate in a snowbank beside the school and turned it in. When I came to collect the plate, the vice principal pulled me into her office.

"Are things going okay?" she asked me.

"Sure, they're fine," I replied.

"Are you sure?" she said. "We know that Jason has been bothering you."

"I'm okay," I said again, eager to move on to class.

She gave me a sideways look and I knew she wasn't convinced. "Well, we're all a little concerned about your safety."

It turned out the vice principal had spoken with Jason after noticing how he stalked me in the hallways, and had told him to leave me alone. Before I left the office, I agreed to watch my back, and to have a friend accompany me to classes for the next few weeks.

Jason decided it was better not to bother me at school, but he still called my home even though my stepfather had forbidden him to. If anyone but me answered the phone, Jason hung up. When I answered, I let him grovel and tell me how much he loved me before I too hung up the phone. There was a part of me that could not let go of his devotion, the part of me that lingered on the line.

Valentine's Day arrived with a blizzard and a call from a florist in a neighboring town who needed directions. My mother answered the phone.

"Send them back," she told the confused person on the other end of the line. "We don't want them."

I knew the flowers must be for me, and I knew who had ordered them. I answered Jason's call a half-hour later.

"Why'd you send the roses back to me?" he whined through the receiver.

"I didn't want them," I whispered my lie.

"But I sent you thirteen. It cost me a lot of money. They were all red, with a white one for forgiveness," Jason pleaded.

I hesitated, while I thought how nice it would have been to have roses from a boy who thought he loved me, even if it was Jason. The only roses I had ever received were from my stepfather, after his anger towards me led to guilt.

"I'm not taking you back," I told him.

I kept the carnations for Valentine's Day, though, along with his hand-scribbled notes that said, "I love you!!" beside his name. The flowers were sent through the school as a fundraising opportunity, and I kept the speckled red-and-white flowers in a vase in my room and hid the notes in a box in my closet. They weren't the only carnations I had received, so it was easy enough to evade my family's suspicious looks.

Shortly after I broke up with Jason, I befriended Sally, the girl with the milky gray glasses perpetually slimed with spit balls in grade school. Now that I had myself become a victim of almost unbearable humiliation, losing a lot of friends and my popularity in the process, I understood how Sally must have felt in grade school. I was also realizing my guilt and remorse for the part I played in Sally's tormented years.

In the summer before the eleventh grade, Sally introduced me to a boy named Shawn, her boyfriend Brett's best friend. I liked the idea of starting fresh with a boy who didn't know me, a boy from another town and school.

On our first date, we doubled with Sally and Brett. The four of us met up on the shores of Lake Winnipesaukee to attend a dance for teens on the Mount Washington cruise ship. When I first saw Shawn, I was under-whelmed. I thought his nose was too large, and I didn't care for the way he kept bragging about all of his accomplishments. As the night progressed, and I danced with Shawn, I decided I kind-of liked the pale green of his eyes and the solid feel of his body beneath his shirt. Like Jason, he told me I was pretty.

After the dance was over, Sally wanted to take a walk on the beach. The moon that evening was unimpeded by the atmosphere, and a wavy path of white light stretched like the tail of a specter across the water toward the shore. It was a warm night and Sally wanted to go swimming, so she stripped off her pants and start walking into the water.

"Come on Alethea, come with me," she called over her shoulder. Sally's voice teased while her smiling face glowed against the blackness.

I didn't dare.

"Chicken," Sally taunted before she dove into the path of light, her body becoming a pearl of the moon. While Sally swam, I imagined how it would feel to strip free of my clothes and dive into the cool dark water while two boys I barely knew watched me from the shore. It was a thrilling thought that made my heart race with possibility, but instead I watched Sally with my feet firmly planted in the sand.

My first date alone with Shawn also started out on water. We took a canoe to a small island on a lake near his house. I sat in the bow of the boat, while Shawn steered and directed from the stern. I was the weaker, less experienced rower, which he took no pains in pointing out to me, as we paddled to the secluded island.

Alone, on the sun-soaked rocks of the island, Shawn kissed me and told me how pretty he thought I was, and my heart began to soften in his embrace. He was, at least, a good kisser. Too soon the sun began to descend behind the pines, and I told him we should probably head to shore.

"I have to babysit at six," I said.

"I don't want to go yet. I'm having a nice time, aren't you?" Shawn pleaded firmly.

I was torn. Although I didn't want to disappoint Shawn, I also didn't want to break my commitment.

I arrived home after six-thirty with a stomach filled with guilt. I hadn't called my parents at Shawn's to tell them I would be late before I drove home. I had no excuse.

"We lost track of time," I mumbled the lie when I stepped through the door, careful not to meet my parents' disappointing eyes.

"We were canoeing, and didn't have access to a phone. I didn't have my watch," I added.

My mother and stepfather made me sit and eat the plate of tepid rice and chicken they had saved for me after I called the parents of the little girl I had promised to watch. It was the first time in my five years of babysitting that I was going to be late, and I felt horrible. Each bite of rice turned to paste inside my mouth. The chicken was impossible to chew. I had no one to blame but myself.

The second time Shawn took me out in a canoe, we paddled on the currents of the Pemigewasset River. Again I took the bow, while Shawn navigated from the stern. It was a cool fall day, and I was wearing my favorite sweatshirt with "Harvard" printed in maroon letters on the front. The school I secretly dreamed of attending in two years. Well, not entirely secretly, my stepfather had bought me the shirt, thrilled at the prospect of having a daughter attend an Ivy League school.

The river was rushing to get ahead of us, and I wasn't having much fun while I tried to follow Shawn's orders to help him steer the ca-

noe around the rocks jutting out of the water. The current, it seemed, was against us, and together Shawn and I could not find a way to work with it. I grew hot from exertion, and during a lull I took off my sweatshirt and threw it behind me.

"Left! Left! Go left," Shawn shouted his directions from the back.

"No, you're not doing it right! Paddle harder!" Shawn made no attempt to hide his frustration.

Eventually our paddles ended up on the same side, and the river, in its rush, pushed us over. When my feet met the bumpy bottom of the riverbed, I felt the numbing cold of the water, and the strength of its force as it tried to suck me under. The muscles in my legs flexed in their efforts to keep me rooted, while I struggled with Shawn to right the canoe.

"See what you've done!" he reprimanded me.

For a fleeting moment I thought how easy it would be to let go. To release my legs from their hold and allow the river's body to carry me downstream and away from Shawn. Instead, I held fast, and eventually we righted the canoe and retrieved the oars. My sweatshirt was nowhere to be found.

"Forget about it," Shawn told me, "It's just a shirt."

He was wrong. To me, the sweatshirt was a dream that now seemed fated not to come true. As we paddled to the shore, weighed down by silence and our wet clothes, I began to question my decision to date this boy who was starting to remind me too much of my stepfather.

That day on the river, after we retrieved the canoe and dragged it to shore, Shawn and I rode back to his house in his uncle's truck without speaking to each other. Instead, while I sat hugging the door feeling cold and bitter, Shawn and his uncle chatted like they were enjoying a fine summer's day. When we got to his house, I headed for my car.

"Wait," he told me. "I'll dry our clothes. You can't go home like that. You'll get sick."

I weighed my options before I followed him inside. As my clothes turned in the dryer, I sat on a stool in Shawn's kitchen wearing a pair of his shorts and one of his sweatshirts. I watched him as he heated a can of tomato soup on the stove.

The next time I saw Shawn, he surprised me with roses. It was the second day of the school year, and I wasn't sure if the roses were to remind me I was his girlfriend, or to show me he was sorry. Perhaps it was a little of both.

Despite our moments of peace, I never stopped feeling, in that year with Shawn, like he was trying to mold me into his ideal of a perfect girlfriend. Once, when we were on a date, swimming, he studied me while I contemplated a dive.

"You could be a model," Shawn told me as he surveyed my form.

Later, as I dried in the sun beside him he rubbed his hand up and down my leg, "Why don't you shave your thighs?" he asked.

"Because you can barely see the hairs," I said, "They're blond."

"Oh," he pouted, "I wish you would."

I contemplated Shawn's words for about a week, and then one day in the shower I let the razor feel the length of my legs.

Another day, when Shawn saw a copy of my school picture from sophomore year, he proclaimed, "You look good with a lot of make-up."

The "frosty" image Shawn admired embarrassed me. I now thought, as my parents' did, that I looked ridiculous with my permed hair, blue-shadowed eyes and pearly pink lip gloss. I couldn't look like that again, not even for Shawn.

Eventually Shawn and I grew tired of his efforts to change me. We both knew we were really looking for someone else. I still wanted Shawn's nose to be smaller, and for him to dress a little cooler. And, I wanted Shawn to stop acting like he was better than me.

Shawn, on the other hand, was still looking for the perfect girl who wasn't me. One day he stopped the car on the side of the road, just down the hill from Margot's.

"I have something to tell you," he said, and my heart skipped a beat.

Okay, I thought, this is it. He's finally breaking up with me.

I waited while Shawn struggled with his thoughts.

"Do you ever think about going out with other people at school?"

"No," I said. It was the truth. I had no intention of ever dating another boy from my school.

Shawn paused again before he offered his confession, "Sometimes, when I'm sitting in class. I think about the pretty girls in the room, and what it would be like to date them."

I didn't know how to respond. *Who doesn't check out other people,* I wanted to say, *but why the heck are you telling me this?* Turns out Shawn didn't want to break up with me, he just wanted to lighten the load of the guilt he was feeling by confessing his secret crushes.

Shawn and I continued to date until the following summer, and sometimes we managed to get along. We had the distance of our separate schools, and while Shawn was applying to colleges, I applied to attend the Advanced Studies Program for upcoming seniors at St. Paul's School in Concord, New Hampshire. I was thrilled when I got in, even though it would mean six weeks away from home, and from Shawn, except on the weekends when visitors were allowed.

A boy from Manchester

wanted to know
My heart

doubt
tried
to decipher
romance

As we
slipped
inside
love

M y first week of summer school at St. Paul's was miserable. I felt embarrassingly unprepared for advanced biology amid a classroom of competent peers, and overwhelmed trying to meet new friends. When the weekend arrived, I called my parents and told them I wanted to go home.

"Stick it out, Alethea," they said. "We know you can do it."

I did, and in a landscape of brick buildings nobly placed amid rolling green grass and weeping willows, I spent the next five weeks falling in love. Four days after I phoned my parents wanting to go home, I met a boy from Manchester. He was, I thought at first, too good to be true. As it turned out, half the girls in my dorm thought the same, and we all wanted to know more about the tan, dark haired boy who was studying ecology. My friend Katie, who roomed upstairs from me, took on the role of match-maker, proudly proclaiming she went to the same high school as the sought-after boy. Katie became the girl to know, giving each of us hope with the news that her friend was at the tail-end of a rocky relationship. Emboldened by the safety of having a boyfriend back home, I decided I had nothing to lose.

Katie introduced me, along with a group of five other adoring girls, to her handsome classmate on the Fourth of July. That night, I wore a black dress covered in Hawaiian flowers, lent to me by a new friend. Our dorm was attending an ice-cream social hosted by the boys of Clark for the girls of Manville, and I was over-dressed, but that was the point.

Katie's friend was seated on a plastic box in the hallway with his teal windbreaker zipped loosely around his neck, looking bored and irresistible as we made our entrance. He acknowledged our presence with a slight turn of his head and mumbled a "Hi" as Katie made the introductions to his fan club.

"This," she proudly announced, "is Dave." My heart skipped a beat when he looked at me, lingering with his eyes before he turned them away. I hardly thought about the name he shared with my father.

The next day, Katie revealed that Dave was interested in one of the girls from our dorm. "He said she has blond hair," she told us during biology class. We all turned to survey each other, then rested our eyes on the only true blond in the group. It wasn't me. My hair, although highlighted from the sun, was definitely brown.

Later, at lunch, Katie waltzed over to the table where Dave was sitting, and asked him to point out the girl he liked. My friends and I cast furtive glances between giggles at Katie and Dave, who, in turn, looked back at us. When she returned, Katie came over to me. "He likes you," she announced. I was as stunned as the girl beside me. "No way, are you sure? She doesn't even have blond hair," my lunch companion replied.

"I'm sure. He's a guy. They don't really know what's blond," Katie laughed and smiled.

Three days later, Katie arranged for us to meet at the library. I didn't tell Shawn, convincing myself that it was not a true date, as Dave and I were there to study. While Dave tried to work on an essay for the required English class, I made a lame attempt to decipher my biology homework. Not much studying got accomplished as we sat flirted on the over-sized chairs in the tiny loft study nook.

Feeling brave with nothing to lose, I teased Dave, testing him for signs that he was like the other boys I had dated.

"Why did you choose ecology?" I asked, trying not to blush. "I heard it's the easiest course here."

"Because I didn't want to spend my summer inside."

"So what's your essay about?"

"Hiking Blueberry Mountain behind my family's lake cottage."

Oh great, he's a rich kid, I thought, but said instead. "Do you need any help with it? I can look it over if you want. I'll read your essay if you'll help me with my biology homework."

"Sure, if you really don't mind reading it." Dave sounded genuinely grateful for my offer to proof his essay.

After I finished, and pointed out the various changes I would make to his essay, Dave gave me a sideways glance. "Maybe you can go there with me some day. It's my favorite place."

My heart skipped a beat as I studied the cute freckle on his left thumb, and continued skipping through the next four and a half weeks. Dave, as it turned out, was nothing like the other boys I had dated. He showed no signs of being interested in other girls, nor did he seem to want to change anything about me.

Although Dave broke up with his girlfriend, and I with Shawn, soon after our date at the library, I found myself growing anxious as summer school approached its end. Did Dave, I wondered, still intend to date me, or was this just a summer romance?

The night before the program's graduation ceremony, there was a dance outside the gymnasium complex. As Dave held me during a slow song, he whispered in my ear, "Do you want to go up to the fields?"

We slipped away, unnoticed.

Under a ceiling of stars, Dave and I talked, kissed, and listened to the muted music filtering through the trees. It felt as though we had the world to ourselves, and as Eric Clapton's "Wonderful Tonight" reached through the inky darkness to play inside our ears, Dave began to sing to me. His voice was a whisper, and a little off-key, but that didn't matter to me. For the first time in my life, I felt like I was good enough for someone else's love. Someone who didn't want to change anything about me.

The next day, Dave and I graduated from our respective programs. At the ceremony, I found myself thinking about the previous evening, wishing it had never ended. We still had not talked about what would happen after we went home. I was afraid to ask, not wanting to assume too much. After everyone received their diplomas, I looked over at Dave, who was standing by his family, while I stood with mine. He smiled, waved, then walked over and handed me a slip of paper.

"Here's my number," he told me before he asked for mine in return. "I hope we can see each other soon," he added before I introduce him to my family, then together, we walked over to meet his. We left the auditorium holding hands, while Dave's little brother ran ahead of us, turning around every few feet to grin and take our picture.

My senior year wasn't perfect, but it was my best year of school since the seventh grade. I continued to excel academically and athletically, and I now had a boyfriend that brought envy and admiration from my classmates. Although I still blushed often, I no longer walked the halls feeling paranoid and self-conscious. Even my family loved Dave. That is, the family who knew of him.

I hadn't seen my father since his last visit east, when I was fourteen. When he called every couple of weeks to check-in with me and Tara, I grew more and more irritated and curt with my responses. I rolled my eyes toward my mother across the room, and she, in turn, rolled hers. It was going on four years since I had seen him, and in my mind my father had proven that he didn't, like my mother always told us, really care about me and Tara.

I was angry and hurt, although I didn't allow myself to see the hurt caused by a father I thought never loved me. I wanted retribution. I wanted revenge. I wanted him erased from my life. So I decided I would get rid of the name that never felt like it belonged to me. The name my father he had given me because he couldn't accept that I was born a girl.

I had always like Tara's middle name, Stacy. It had an airy sound reminding me of wings. Of grace.

"At least," I told her, "you got a girl's name."

Tara, though, never liked it, and with the encouragement of our mother, we decided to change our middle names. One day, the three of us made a list of women descended from the maternal side of our family. When we got to Elizabeth, the name shared by my grandmother and great-grandmother, I took it for my own. Elizabeth. The name of a queen. Strong, simple, and beautiful.

Many years later I would research the origin of my chosen name, along with the one I had traded it for. Derived from Hebrew, Elizabeth means "I am God's daughter." Eamon, in Old English, "The Protector of Wealth." At eighteen, I didn't know that one day I would cease being a protector of family secrets; this shroud of wealth each child must bear. I didn't realize that one day I would embrace my spirit and its creator in a journey of profound and deep healing.

On that day when I was eighteen, I was thinking about my birth and the father who had given me a boy's name. I was thinking about graduation, Margot, and Ann, anticipating the satisfaction of seeing my full name appear, without shame, in fancy red script next to the names of my classmates.

When I stood before the judge he smiled at me, lifting his head for just a moment, from the certificate in front of him.

"Is there a reason why you are changing your middle name?" he asked. I assumed it was a standard question by the casual tone of his voice.

"I've never liked it," I replied.

That was it. With no more words, I watched this stranger erase the boy that was never born

A few months later, on a windy, June afternoon, I stood on a podium in front of my classmates in a white robe with a gold sash draped over my shoulders. I was graduating ahead of Margot and Ann. I was graduating ahead of all of my classmates, but one. As salutatorian, I had earned the honor of giving a speech. I looked at the rows of friends and relatives waiting to hear me speak, and took a long breath of air into my lungs, letting it fill my cells with the crisp bite of new beginnings.

I didn't care that I was not graduating first in my class of eighty-six. The valedictorian, Melanie, had worked hard for, and more than deserved the honor. I was satisfied with second. I was proud of what I had achieved during my tumultuous adolescent years. The last four of which had been a lesson in adversity, but also in perseverance.

Now, facing the sun and the audience queued along the grass, I looked forward to a new beginning. In a few months, I would be heading to Maine to attend Bowdoin College with the boy I had fallen in love with at summer school.

On this day I bore no shame. There was no need to hide behind the brown paper bag I had been gifted by my peers at Class Night the previous evening as a joke for my tendency to blush. I had already recycled my "gift" before I stepped for the last time outside the doors of my high school with eyes turned toward a future waiting to be sculpted by my hands. I didn't want to look back at what I had left behind. My telescope was pointed to a place called change.

I even titled my salutatory address "Changes." With my back to my classmates, I talked about the past and new beginnings, using an old stone bench covered with ivy I would often pass by and sit upon while at St. Paul's as my metaphor. The bench was old and gray, the ivy that clung to its back growing denser with each passing year. For six weeks, that summer, it provided a seat upon which for me to rest and reflect, just as it did for the many students who passed through St. Paul's each year. It was a constant, unresisting witness to changing forces.

I had worked hard to craft my speech, going through several drafts with my advisor before I was satisfied with the result. With each spoken word I felt the power of my voice. Under the privacy of my robe, my body trembled, but the vibration of my words rippled through the silent audience with strength and conviction. My closing remarks were met with loud applause.

A growing emptiness

I saw the girl with feathered hair
beside her grandmother
a face of lines I could
not read. A halo of white curls hover above loss
click the shutter and

remember forgotten

grief
I thought I was
fine

On my nineteenth birthday I traveled to Brunswick, Maine tucked between my mother and the passenger side door of my stepfather's truck. Feelings of nervous excitement fueled me during the long drive. Although I looked forward to meeting my roommate, I also worried about what she would think of me and my parents. I looked over at my stepfather, with his shaggy beard, red suspenders, and brown work boots. *Why couldn't he have dressed-up a little for the occasion?* I agonized.

As we drove, I prayed the cool August air wafting through his open window would be enough to mask his non-deodorized armpits. Immersed in my thoughts, I hardly paid attention to my parents as they joked about how I had violated their two-hour-by-car limit for college. I wasn't going to Harvard, I didn't even apply, but I knew they were proud that their daughter was going to a "Little Ivy."

Packed into the bed of my stepfather's truck were cardboard boxes filled with everything my parents and I thought I needed for my first year away from home. I had most of my wardrobe, my boom box and tapes, a hot pot, a popcorn popper, and a discarded word processor my stepfather had retrieved for free from the Canterbury dump.

My roommate, Nicky, was already unpacked when I arrived. On the desk beside the door was the phone we would share that year, along with Nicky's new Macintosh computer and a framed photograph of the boy she was in love with back home. Nicky, as I soon found out, was still seventeen. She had graduated from a small private school, and was, like a can of soda pop, sweet and full of bubbles.

When I first met Nicky I liked her, and she seemed to like me. Unfortunately this didn't last, and after a few short months, we learned we had very little, except our anticipated majors, in common. I always tried to go to bed on the early side, somewhere between ten and eleven. In the fall, Nicky chose to pledge a fraternity and often stumbled into the room in the wee hours of the morning, her clothes soiled with her rites of passage.

Nicky was friends with the noisy girls on the other side of our bedroom wall. Girls that reminded me too much of Margot and Ann with their gossip and glee that echoed through the hallways long past the hour I turned out my light. I didn't trust them, just as I began not to trust Nicky, and I found myself swirling back into the eddy of my adolescent insecurities.

I made friends with two quiet girls on our floor. They both came from lower-middle-class families, like mine, and hailed from small New England towns. They were, unlike me and my roommate, well-matched, and I felt like a third-wheel when I would visit them next door. I turned often to Dave, trying to spend most of my non-classroom hours with the boy I loved, a person, I was learning, had no intention of ever turning against me.

My social life beyond Dave was pretty dismal. By November, my roommate and I had stopped talking to each other. In my mind, she had taken up alliances with the girls next door, who seemed to enjoy making my life miserable by partying late into the night, especially when I asked them to be quiet. I felt distrust and suspicion return, along with the feeling that I would never really find a place to fit in.

In the late fall I joined the nordic ski team. I had excelled at this sport during my years at Belmont, and I knew Bowdoin was eager to add me to their team. It only lasted two months, and I never gave myself the chance to race. I left, not because I didn't want to compete, but because I felt I didn't have the means to.

When I ran through the woods training with my teammates before the snow started to fall, I found myself worrying about how I was going to acquire the equipment I needed to race. The team captain pressured me to order two new sets of skis, and in my mind I could not create a way to manifest the hundreds of dollars it was going to cost me to become a competitive college skier. So I quit, using the excuse of my demanding course load when I told my baffled and disappointed teammates and family. I didn't feel I had the right to ask my parents for money they didn't have to buy the skis I needed, and I was too ashamed to tell my wealthy teammates. To me, it was one more sign that I didn't belong.

***

One day, before Thanksgiving break of my first year in college, the phone rang on my roommate's desk. She answered the call, and handed the receiver to me. I pulled the coil of wire toward the couch while I listened to the voice of my mother on the other end of the line.

"I'm calling to let you know that Grammie Fischer died," my mother said after we exchanged our hellos. Her voice, I noted, was devoid of affect. I felt the walls of my chest contract, closing the door around my heart.

"How did she die?" I asked.

"I don't know," my mother replied impatiently. "Dave called last night to pass on the news. You know how he is."

I could tell my mother didn't want to talk about it anymore. She had fulfilled her obligation of letting me know my grandmother had died, and was ready to move onto other subjects. So I let her.

As I half-listened to my mother's debriefing of town events that had occurred during my absence, inside of my mind I saw a young

157

girl with feathered brown hair and deep blue eyes sitting beside the ghost of a grandmother.

While my mother talked, indifferent to how I might feel about this loss, I thought of the last time I saw Grammie. I recalled the bend of her body, leaning into mine as we peered into my father's camera together. I saw her face with its large brown eyes surrounded by the lines of a full life I barely knew. Above, a halo of tight white curls hovered above her head. I clicked the shutter of memory closed and hung up the phone.

"Are you okay?"

In that moment of remembering I had forgotten I was not alone in the room. I turned to look at my roommate's face filled with concern, and realized, with a twinge of annoyance, that she knew as much about Grammie's death as I did.

"My grandmother died," I said in a voice devoid of emotion.

"I'm so sorry," she replied, outwardly appearing more upset than me. "Is there anything I can do?"

I looked into my roommate's face, which was filled with the grief she imagined was inside of me. A grief that would have filled her if her own grandmother had passed away. My chest tightened in response. No, there was nothing she could do for me, I thought. I was fine.

"It's okay," I told her. "We were never close."

My roommate looked shocked, and I knew she thought I had a heart emptied of love. In some ways, it was. In my mind, I was still holding onto the belief that I had erased Grammie from my life when she had ceased sending me birthday and Christmas cards a few years after Tara and I stopped going out to Oregon. I would not allow myself to feel grief that she was now gone forever, even though I could feel pressure building against the dam behind my eyes.

The man I tried to erase

has a
face smiling with reunion
read my turmoil
I wanted to
capture comfort

but I didn't
know how to
forget

Three weeks before my twenty-second birthday, I flew to Oregon with my mother and sister to visit my grandparents. When I stepped into the Portland airport arrival room, my eyes met the man I had tried to erase from memory. As I registered his unexpected presence, I felt the energy of resentment surge through me. I looked at my mother and saw my emotions mirrored in her eyes.

I couldn't ignore my father. There he was beside my cousin Laura, just like old times, their faces smiling with reunion. I wonder now what they read of my turmoil when they saw me. People have often told me I wear my emotions on my face. That day, though, I didn't care. I cared only that they were there, uninvited by us. I had wanted this trip to Oregon to be different. My primary desire was to capture the happy comfort of my grandparents' world one more time.

When my father embraced me, I felt the arms of a stranger. His face, I noted, looked too much like mine, but I couldn't read the map of lines on his forehead that had deepened and grown in the seven-and-a-half years since I had last seen him. I didn't know where to begin. I didn't know where to end. I wasn't ready to travel down paths I had tried so hard to forget. Instead, I raised my ready guard and waited for his kiss to leave the smooth skin of my cheek.

My mother stood uncomfortably beside me while I hugged her ex-husband and my cousin.

"Hi," I could hear her anger through the strain of her smile. Her eyes looked past the tops of their two heads. Her feet shuffled restlessly, wanting to move.

"How are you doing?" my father replied as he looked my mother full in the face. His smile, genuine and unrestrained.

In that moment, I realized my father still loved my mother. Even after twenty years, there was an ownership to his gaze, as

161

though he had not fully let her go. I knew my mother felt it too; I could feel her body cringe as it pulled away from the energy of his stare.

My mother was annoyed with her mother before they even had a chance to greet each other. It was clear, by process of deduction, that my grandmother was the cause of my father and cousin being at the airport. The time of our arrival was something we had decided not to share with him when Tara and I told our father we were coming out. My grandmother, it had become apparent, had done it for us.

Before we flew west, Tara and I agreed to spend one day out of the eight with our father and his side of our family. That was it. It was a day that we were, for the most part, dreading. Even though we were gathering at our favorite Aunt, Linda's, house, we would be among family we had not seen since we were children. There were even some we had never met.

My grandparents footed the bill for our flights, sending us the plane tickets as a way to invite the daughter and granddaughters they hadn't seen in nearly eight years back into their lives. This time, we would sleep in their new, modest two-bedroom retirement house in Keizer. The hour drive to Keizer held the strains of tension formed at the airport, but I tried to focus on the pleasure of being reunited with my mother's family and the state of my birth. I watched the landscape through the window of the car, matching it with pieces from my memory. I noted the patchwork of ivy and grass along the freeway, and searched for the snowy peak of Mt. Hood that hovered over the horizon like the tipped chalice of a god.

When we got to my grandparents' house, Poppy proudly gave us a tour. The foyer, like their house on Mt. Scott, was paved with local rock. It was bumpy and beautiful, and as I walked the length of its surface the comforts of the past returned to me. The living room, although smaller than their former living room, contained the floral sofas of my memory, along with my favorite velvet chair, the color of emerald moss. Photographs of my aunts and uncles with their piercing blue eyes lined the walls of hallways. When I passed my mother's face, I almost saw my own.

That night, and for the next six nights, I slept in the spare bedroom with my mother. My sister, because of her tendency to snore, was relegated to the larger sofa in the open-concept living room. She got less sleep than I did, being subjected to Poppy's early rising, but I would have rather traded places with her if I could.

Each night, while we lay together in the double bed, with just a wall separating us from her parents, my mother rehashed the day's events. My cousin, just a few months younger than me, appeared through my mother's words immature and spoiled. I saw her standing at the admission gate of the state fair that we had attended earlier in the day, hesitating to open her wallet after my mother paid for three people, and not four. I felt sorry for my cousin, and also embarrassed that my mother had, once again, refused to part with money. But, as my mother spoke in the darkened bedroom I didn't disagree with her words.

While my mother talked, a memory stored years before came stubbornly into focus inside of my mind. I saw my fourteen-year-old self with my friend Jean at the local mall one day. It was lunchtime, and we were meeting my mother at Arby's to eat with her before we went home. When we arrived at the restaurant, my mother was already standing in line, waiting for us. She checked out first, paying only for her sandwich and soft drink before she walked to an open booth with her tray. I stood with Jean, behind her, my face flushed red, and whispered hurriedly into my friend's ear that I would buy her lunch. "It's okay," she said as she fumbled in her wallet for money she hadn't planned on using.

163

When this memory left, another one came to take its place. My mother and I were driving a friend of mine from Belmont, Jill, home after a sleepover. It was well past noon, and during the ride Jill wondered aloud if we were going to stop for lunch, as we hadn't eaten before we left my house.

"I don't think so," I whispered back, wanting to sink through the cushions of the car and disappear. My mother, in the front seat, acted like she didn't hear.

Midway through the week, my mother revisited her own childhood before we fell asleep. "I've retrieved a forgotten memory," she told me as a I lay beside her.

"It's about my brother, Paul," she continued, and I felt the familiar creep of discomfort crawl inside my body, seeking release as I listened.

"He came into my bedroom one night," my mother said. As she spoke, my mind filled with the image of my mother as a young girl trying to fall asleep. Her brother, quietly entering her room. I felt his hands, as though my mother's body were mine, sliding under her covers, finding the cotton cloth of her nightgown, and pulling it up. My skin felt the sin of his fingers as he explored his sister's flesh. This memory, like so many others shared by my mother, was now also mine.

My mother's childhood memories of incest and abuse were, by now, so tangled with my own that I sometimes forgot that they were not mine. What would it take, I began to wonder, to break free of this legacy of perversion that began before my mother was born? A legacy of memories she began sharing with me when I was just a child. I knew that my uncle had a reason to search his sister's body for pleasure, as I had grown up hearing the stories of his step-great-grandfather, the man I called Stauvic, molesting him when he was a child. Just as he had molested my grandmother when she was a girl.

The discomfort of my mother's memories was still clinging to me at the end of the week, on the day Tara and I set aside to spend with our paternal relatives. That morning, my father arrived to retrieve us from our grandparents' house with his brother Sam. No one offered an explanation as to why Sam and not my father was driving, but when Tara and I looked at each other I knew we were both wondering if our father's license had been revoked. If so, why? Had he been caught with pot, or driving drunk? The possibilities played inside my mind as I reluctantly strapped myself into the backseat.

Sam, it became clear soon after we pulled out of the driveway, didn't want to play the role of chauffeur. Periodically during the

hour it took to get to Portland, my uncle remarked upon the chore of driving, while my father nervously laughed and tried to fill the silence with awkward chatter about his work as a landscaper. When we reached the city, we stopped to pick up a keg of beer and food for the party. While standing in line, commenting about the expense it was costing him to supply food and beverages for the gathering in our honor, my father accepted Tara's offer to help out. I watched as she handed over some of the spending money Poppy had given the three of us at the beginning of the week.

When we arrived at my Aunt Linda's, her lawn was already dotted with people. As I walked up the path to the backyard, I tried to label the children running across the lawn. I recognized first my cousin Kimberly, with her round face and dark eyes. Although she was no longer blond, she still resembled the two-year-old child I had said goodbye to nine years before. The girl playing beside her I knew must be my cousin Kelly, who was also two-years-old the last time I saw her. She seemed too shy, though, to be the tiny girl with brown curls I remembered belting out "Twinkle, Twinkle Little Star" with perfect pitch. Now eleven, Kelly wore round glasses that hid large green eyes. The curly hair of my memory was pulled tight into a ponytail.

Kimberly and Kelly's younger brothers I knew only by deductive reasoning. They had not yet been born when I was last in Oregon. Nick, now nine, was small and dark like his sister, and Tim looked like a boy version of Kimberly. That left the two small girls who hid behind their mother's legs. I didn't know their mother, but I sort-of knew their father, my youngest uncle on my father's side. During our absence, Uncle Jeff had married and now had two daughters of his own, Monica and Stacy.

While my sister and I greeted the shy children who knew us only by name, my cousin Danielle arrived. I noticed first her height, which almost equaled Tara's. As I took in her curly hair, now long, and the dark complexion and eyes of Grammie's Croatian heritage, I recognized the young girl I used to play with. I learned, in those moments beside Danielle and my other cousins, how difficult it is to try to erase a span of time that is nearly half your life. Cousins had been born in my absence, while others had grown into adulthood and married. An uncle had died, and so had Grammie. I had missed each of these events and many more that my paternal family had shared together.

As I stood with my sister, trying make up for lost time with our cousins, our father came over and placed an arm around each of our shoulders.

"I'd like you to meet some people," he said, and we followed dutifully under his embrace.

In a cluster of chairs on the side of the lawn sat a group of smiling strangers, and I realized they must be my father's friends. *Why did he invite them?* I wondered as I thought about the zoo and how it felt to be the object of display when I was a child. A rumble of anger stirred deep inside my belly.

With a tight smile, I shook hands with my father's friends and tried to place their faces in scenes from the past. My memory could not recover the clues I sought, and as I looked at his guests, I wondered what they knew about my life. A life my father had largely been absent from.

While my father beamed with pride from the accolades he received regarding how well my sister and I had turned out, I suppressed the desire to tell them the truth. That this man holding onto our shoulders was almost as much of a stranger to us as they were. That he could lay claim only to the genes we had inherited from him.

On a table, beside my father's friends, I noticed a brown album edged with a thin gold band. The words "Tara and Alethea" were printed on the cover of an unfinished book of our lives. I felt a spark of pleasure as I began to flip through its pages. With my sister beside me, I forgot about the people of the present and immersed myself in images from our past. My mother had only a few photographs from our early childhood, and each of these saved pictures from my father allowed me to add scenes to what I couldn't recover through memory alone. As I flipped through the pages, I never thought about how much the album, compiled with such care, must have meant to the person who made it. A parent who had lived, for most of his children's lives, only with photographs.

After my sister and I finished looking through the album, Tara turned to our father. "Thank you," she said as she started to lift the weight of the book.

My father replied with a nervous laugh mixed with a clearing of his throat, "Uh, you're welcome. I wanted to bring it to show everyone how you've grown over the years." The album was, we both realized, with a mixture of disappointment and embarrassment, not ours to keep.

The remainder of the afternoon passed as all time does, but to me it was a slow and uncomfortable passing. I couldn't wait to return to my grandparents' house. I couldn't wait to be free of the day. The ride back to Keizer stretched out in long, slow miles. The only person who wanted to be in the car was my father. My Uncle Sam, who drove us home, interjected remarks about the distance he had to travel again, and how he had to leave the party too early. My sister and I, sitting silently in the darkened backseat of the car, tried to will the miles away.

Poppy welcomed us through the door when we arrived safely back at our grandparents' home, and Tara and I joined our mother and grandmother in the living room. I took a section of the sofa beside my mother. Tara, one of the cushioned chairs.

"How'd it go?" my mother asked, looking first at Tara and then at me.

As my mother's eyes fixed upon my face, the wall inside me, which I had tried to keep fortified all afternoon, dissolved. My body shook against the soft cushions of the couch, and hot, angry tears spilled from my eyes.

"It was horrible," I replied through sobs. "Horrible."

My mother's face bore a look of anger mixed with satisfaction, while I struggled with emotions that rocked my body and strangled my breath. Soon my sister was crying along with me, leaving our grandparents looking desperate for a means to assuage our grief. I hardly noticed my grandmother leave the room. When she returned, she was carrying two small boxes. She gave one to Tara and one to me.

"I was saving these to give you when you leave," she told us as we opened our gifts of birthstone earrings. For a moment the rage of emotions inside of me quieted, just a little.

After we thanked our grandparents for their gifts, my mind and body returned to anger and hurt, all of which I directed at my father.

On the plane ride home the next day, my anger had transformed into a desire for revenge. I blamed everything on my father. All of the accumulated hurt held inside of me, I decided, was his fault. I held onto my mother's truth that he was the villain in the story of my life. Anger surged within me as I thought about how my father had proudly laid claim to two daughters he hadn't raised. I wanted to take my hand and wipe away the smile of pride I could still see spread across his face from the previous day. I was not his daughter. I never had been. He had, as my mother and stepfather often told me and Tara, no right to call us his own.

On the flight back east, I came up with a plan that I hoped would permanently free me of my turmoil and anger. Once the idea came into my head, I needed to get it out, so I turned to my mother and sister sitting beside me.

"I think we should have dad officially adopt us," I announced.

My mother's face took on the light of the sun. "Oh, that will make him so happy," she said as tears began to fill the corners of her eyes.

I wanted my sister to love my idea, which, once I said it aloud, did not yield the internal relief I had hoped for. Instead, I felt as though I was shoveling dirt over a shallow grave. Tara's face looked slightly shell-shocked.

"What do you think?" I asked her, hoping she would warm to the idea, hoping that together we could find a way to relieve the weight of our past.

"Sure, I guess that's fine with me," she said with a face devoid of light.

My mother assigned my sister the task of contacting a lawyer when we got home. The adoption, we had decided, would be a surprise Christmas gift for my stepfather.

"I had to run around and make phone calls. I didn't even know what I was doing," my sister told me years later as she recalled the memory of trying to obtain the adoption paperwork.

"It was a pain in the ass. And," my sister confessed, "I never really felt like I had a choice."

Her words stung. It was my idea, after all. An idea I too would later question.

When I was twenty-one, though, I felt as sorry for my stepfather as my mother and he did. I still held firmly to the notion that he was our insecure hero. The only father who really loved us and cared enough to be a part of our lives. I believed I was forever in debt to this man who had made the choice to raise me and Tara as his own daughters. I never let myself consider how conditional this agreement was, and how it had cost me the loss of my biological father and extended family in my life growing up. Even though our relationship was not an easy one, I loved my stepfather with a daughter's loyalty. Adoption was my way of showing one father gratitude, while attempting to cut the bond of birth with the other.

At Christmas, Tara, my mom, and I placed the adoption documents in an over-sized envelope topped with a bow. My sister and I presented our gift to our stepfather, who sat in his recliner by the window, while my mother took pictures.

"What is it?" my stepfather asked, sensing the content of the envelope was heavier than its weight, as he turned it over.

My stepfather's eyes filled with tears when he read the papers that had been held inside.

"I love you," I said, the salty water of my emotions spilling from my eyes, sincere in my words. I leaned over to hug and kiss the only man I could remember calling "dad."

Muted

I

chose

to be an accessory to

My mother's marriage
an extension
of her hate
and
joy
a daughter

Who
stumbled on
a path not
hers

In August of 1996, after we graduated from Bowdoin, Dave and I moved into an apartment together in Mansfield, Massachusetts. I was enrolled in a molecular biology, cellular biology and biochemistry Ph.D. program at Brown University, and Dave had accepted a position as a laboratory assistant at Massachusetts General Hospital. Our first year living together in our tiny attic apartment overlooking Main Street had its ups and downs. Most of the downs were due to my unhappiness with being at Brown. For a year I did my best to pretend I was in a place where I belonged, while struggling to muster the enthusiasm to study material that did not hold my interest.

At the end of my first year in the program, I asked for a leave-of-absence with the knowing that I probably would not return. I had tried to fool myself into believing I wanted to be a "doctor" of science. A role that I knew would make my parents, especially my stepfather, proud, but that, I was realizing, did not define my truth. I left Brown with nowhere to go, and no ideas how to get there. I did the only thing I felt capable of doing, I applied to be a lab assistant like Dave, and got hired in a neuro-genetics laboratory across the Charles River.

Another year, plus a half, passed by, and once again I found myself in a place where I didn't belong. Since I was no longer traveling to Providence, Dave and I moved to a second-story apartment in a rough area of Malden, Massachusetts. The geneticist I was working under was planning to retire when my contract with her was up, and being her only assistant, she kept careful tabs on me throughout the day. Obsessive-compulsive by nature, my boss would accuse me of using her labeled pencils, because the eraser, she pointed out to me, was not at an equal ratio to the lead. When I took photographs of my experiments, she often chided me for cutting the white area under the images too much or too little. She liked the empty space, used for writing, precisely 1 1/2 inches, and I didn't like to measure.

One day, I went to see my primary care provider for a routine check-up during my lunch break. Everything looked fine, except my blood pressure. After monitoring it for a few weeks, my doctor decided to do some blood work. The results returned with a diagnosis of hypothyroidism. I had, it appeared, succumbed to the same disease as many of the women on the maternal side of my family, my mother included. Although I was disappointed, assuming that I would have to take a pill for the rest of my life to compensate for my sluggish thyroid gland, I accepted a fate that I attributed only to genetics.

It wouldn't be until many years later, after I transitioned from studying science to metaphysics, that I would make the connection between thyroid disease and the throat chakra, an energy center within our bodies that, when healthy, allows the unimpeded flow of energy from the heart through the throat. When our throat chakra is balanced, we are able to speak our truths without fear. If the energy is trapped for too long, disease can set in. There is a pattern in thyroid disease, I have come to learn, which is woven with more than genetics. It is also tangled with the muted threads of silence; the blocking of one's truth.

More than a decade would pass after my diagnosis, before I would look at my thyroid disease as my body's way of calling attention to an energetic imbalance that afflicts generations of women (and men) afraid to speak their truths with conviction and compassion. In the meantime, I was trying to find security in a city that filled me with insecurities. A placed filled with congestion and smog, where children walked home from school on the same sidewalk as prostitutes. It was a place where tires were stolen from cars during the night.

One day, Dave and I entered the unlocked door leading into the windowless hallway of our apartment building, just like we did every day of the work week. I went up the stairs to the second floor first, and paused at the landing to let my eyes adjust to the lack of light. As I focused on the dark wood of the hallway, I felt the pulse of my heart catch inside my chest.

"We've been robbed," Dave said as he rushed past me, pushing the busted door to our apartment wide open.

It was like I was eight again, only I wasn't.

"Where are the cats?!" I panicked in my search for our beloved pets, Merlin and Tigger. "What if they took them?" I called out when I couldn't find them." What if they're dead? I thought to myself.

In our frantic search, Dave and I opened the door to the closet in the room we used as an office and found our cats huddled together, cowering from fear.

After the cats were safely in our arms, Dave and I took inventory of the wreckage from the robbery. The obvious items were taken — my portable radio, CDs, half the contents of my jewelry box, and my purse, which held my license, credit cards and cash. *Why didn't I take my wallet with me?!* I chided myself as Dave grabbed the phone to start calling the credit card companies, then the police.

"At least they didn't take your pearls," Dave said later as we looked at the spilled contents of my jewelry boxes tipped over on our bed.

It had clearly been a hasty job, or the robbers were idiots. The strings of real pearls, gifts from Dave, were still inside the glass box, as was the sapphire pendant he had given to me for Christmas. Instead, the thieves had stolen jewelry from my stepfather, gifted over the years for birthdays and Christmas. Small semiprecious stones on

175

silver chains and bracelets, as well as a string of fake pearls from an aunt.

The fact that it could have been much worse was little comfort. For the second time in my life, I felt the violation of a home invasion. The fear-filled child inside of me had returned, and as I sat with Dave and the police at the kitchen table, I erupted into tears. The officers looked embarrassed by my display, making me feel foolish. In this town, burglary was not exactly a rare event.

"It's unlikely we'll recover any of your stuff," they told us. "But, we'll let you know if we do."

I found their demeanor to be callous and cold. Weeks later, a police officer called to tell me my license was recovered. "What about the

rest of our stuff?" I asked with a glimmer of hope. "Was any of it found?"

"No, only the license," I was told. "Someone was trying to impersonate you. We have to keep it here for evidence, though. You'll have to get a new one."

The case was closed.

A few months later, Dave asked me to marry him during a trip to Montreal. In the nine months leading up to the ceremony, I never considered inviting my father or any of my birth relatives, aside from my grandparents, to our wedding. My mother only wanted her parents invited, and I didn't argue with her wishes. My stepfather, in turn, insisted upon inviting most of his entire extended family, as well as several of my parents' friends. In many ways it was as much their celebration as it was mine and Dave's. Dave and I had even agreed to have our wedding outside of their home, like my sister had done two years earlier.

I knew if we didn't have our wedding there, my parents would be crushed. Besides, Dave and I couldn't afford a lavish celebration.

176

My contract in the laboratory had ended, and the researcher I was working under retired after my departure. I was working as a substitute teacher, while trying to decide what I was going to do with my life. Dave, who was finishing up his research assistant job, was heading off to medical school in less than a year. Money, for us, was tight.

We also chose the same honeymoon destination as my sister and her husband. Secretly, I dreamed of flying somewhere exotic and romantic, like Hawaii, but two nights at the Balsam's Grand Resort in Dixville Notch, New Hampshire would have to do. My parents, like they had for my sister's wedding, contributed about $500 toward our wedding by paying for the flowers, the cake, and the material for my dress, which my mother made, as she had my sister's. My step-grandparents, who were frequent customers at a brewing shop, enthusiastically offered to cover the cost of making Chianti and Pinot Grigio for our guests. Dave's parents hosted the rehearsal dinner at Canterbury Shaker Village, and we covered the remainder of expenses. Our entire wedding, including the honeymoon, cost about $5,000.

The day before my wedding, my stepfather and I drove to the coast in his pick-up and filled white sheetrock buckets with hundreds of long-stemmed roses from a wholesale grower. I had little say on the colors that could be clipped, but I was only mildly disappointed. There were plenty of pink roses, the color I had chosen for my bridesmaids' dresses, as well as several yellows, whites and reds. My custom order teardrop bouquet of ivory blooms with a sprinkling of pale pink turned out to be enormous. I was thrilled with the excess of flowers we had purchased, and gave little thought to the time it would take to make arrangements to decorate the tables and the surrounding area. My mind instead was focused on the growing heat, and how I was going to keep the blooms from withering.

Canterbury, being a small town, has its advantages. The owner of the center store kindly agreed to store my roses in his coolers overnight. Still, I worried about the temperature. Would the roses now be too cold? On the morning of my wedding, when my stepfather and I went to retrieve the buckets, all was well.

I loved my gown almost as much as my roses. Months before my wedding, my mother and I went shopping for fabric, and after visiting several stores, settled on cream-colored silk and lace embroidered with flowers along the hem. When I tried on the finished dress, I felt like I had walked out of a Victorian photograph. Later, I would be grateful for having chosen a simple gown with little density, held with straps barely wider than spaghetti.

Dave and I hired a young newspaper photographer to take pictures, and my brother-in-law offered to be the videographer. We found an inexpensive DJ to play music under the tent for the reception, and a college flutist, a keyboardist and Dave's cousin created a tiny band for the ceremony. Dave and I spent the bulk of our money on food, choosing a caterer that assembled a masterpiece of dishes to compliment Dave's Greek and Italian heritage, including eggplant musacca, chicken and garlic scampi, and lamb and pepper kabobs.

I awoke early the morning of our wedding, having spent the night at my parents' house, to arrange roses in vases, and punch buds into styrofoam balls for topiaries. My mother took charge of making a hanging orb of pink roses to tie with thick ribbon in the center of the copper arch my stepfather had fashioned to replace the deteriorating wooden one from my sister's wedding.

My bridesmaids, college friends Lila and Larissa, along with Tara, my Matron-of-Honor, rolled up their sleeves and spent the morning helping me to arrange the nearly endless supply of roses into centerpieces. My maternal grandmother sat under the tent, sheltered from the growing heat of the sun, folding thick ivory napkins into fans. Dave and my stepfather laid down a plywood dance floor, and stocked a Coca Cola cooler, borrowed from the center store, with ice and drinks under the tent.

By noon the temperature outside had almost reached its record-breaking peak of ninety-seven degrees. The only wind that afternoon came from the industrial-sized fans my stepfather and his brothers had lugged inside the tents. There were moments during the day when I looked at the wither of the flowers on the arch, and in the pots around the tent, and when I gazed with guilt at the sweat making tiny rivers down the side of my husband's face, that made me wish we had opted for an air-conditioned banquet hall.

Two days before the wedding, after checking the forecast, Dave's father had called us to see if we would be willing to change the site of our wedding to an air-conditioned facility. He even offered to pay for it. My soon-to-be father-in-law was just two weeks out of bypass surgery, but I refused to relent. Everything for the wedding was set. I couldn't fathom the work it would take to call all of the guests, many of whose numbers I didn't have, and find a new location in which to get married. Not to accommodate one guest, even if it was Dave's father.

Instead, my parents rearranged their office into an air-conditioned sitting room with a window-view of the day's events. He watched his son get married from the seat of a rocking chair, peering through the paned window that overlooked the back yard.

By 3:15 p.m., the heat outside had peaked, and the clematis vines were drooping down the sides of the copper arch, trying to find their way to cooler ground. The groom-to-be, the best man, the father-of-the-bride, and two topless flower girls and their father had taken refuge in the pond in front of the house. I was in an airless bedroom upstairs with my patient step-aunt, who was rearranging my hair for the second time into curls and roses. The guests were due to arrive at 4:00 p.m.

At 3:30 p.m. I began to panic and sent my sister outside to order the swimmers to get dressed in their formal attire. "We should have ordered shorts," my husband would later remark, but I stubbornly wanted the formality of pants even though it was a garden wedding. The guests who arrived in shorts made me grimace.

Days after my wedding, Larissa marveled, "You were the only person who made it through the day looking fresh and smelling like a rose."

The heat, in truth, never bothered me that day. I was determined to make the best of my wedding. Nothing was going to stand in my way, not even the unrelenting sun.

When the formal dances were over, Dave disappeared into the house to visit with his father. He brought with him drinks and plates of food. I tried not to think of the people missing, while I stole a pink rose from a nearby table, tucked the thorn-less stem between my teeth, and led a queue of willing guests in a conga line through the dusky, gradually cooling air.

At 9:00 p.m., after the last guests had departed and we had cleaned up under the tent, Dave and I packed into our car and headed north. We stopped at the Three Rivers House Inn in North Woodstock to spend the night and to shorten our drive the next day. When we ar-rived, I filled my arms with my bouquet and wedding dress, attempting to ignore the life-sized wooden moose on the lawn while I navigated my way to the front door. When we got inside, I did my best to over-look the flowers papered to the wall and the rustic furniture. It was not the grand room my imagination had designed for my wedding night, but it would have to do. In the morning, after breakfast in a dining room that housed another (fake) moose, we drove the rest of the way north to the Balsams Grand Resort.

When our three days at the Balsams were over, Dave and I made our way home, stopping by my parents' house to retrieve our cats and wedding gifts. My stepfather was mowing the lawn when we pulled into the driveway, and when he saw our car he shut off the Gravely and came over to greet us. I knew by the missing smile on his face that something was wrong. The residue of happiness from our brief honeymoon vanished as my stepfather opened his mouth to speak.

"There's an ice bill that needs to be paid at the store," he said. "We need to figure out how we're going to take care of it."

Dad

I
visit
the ocean

Wild
to capture childhood. walk
the sand open
to visit birth
I watch the tide wash the walls of
thought and erase

only to remember
he was there, present in the void, a missing gap
that

fills the vast, dark body of

Truth

A year after we were married, Dave and I flew to Oregon to celebrate our first wedding anniversary. I wanted to show my husband the state of my birth, but I wasn't ready to introduce him to all of its people. During our visit, we stayed with my grandparents at their home in Keizer, except for our anniversary night spent at an inn beside the ocean.

As we drove the long coastline, I tried to recapture he happier memories of my childhood. In Bandon, we walked the sand dunes before we headed north into Newport to see the Aquarium that had opened after I stopped going out to visit my father. The bloated sea lions, I noted, were still strewn along the rocky shores of Strawberry Hill. Later, as I watched the tide washing the walls of Devil's Churn, I thought about how slowly time erodes and erases.

Even though I traveled the same paths of my childhood, retracing the long drives of the past with my husband beside me, I tried only to remember the landscape. My father, I told myself, was an unfortunate piece of my history that I had long ago thrown away. Yet he was there, present always in the form of a void, like a missing gap in a jigsaw puzzle that cannot be over-looked, no matter how hard one tries to be satisfied with an incomplete scene.

I focused my attention on the beauty of Oregon: the moss covered trees that filled forests hiding silver falls, and the vast, dark body of the sea rolling over the pale relenting sand. Before me was a landscape where limits were stretched to create nearly impossible beauty. Peaks of earth pushed summer snow to touch the tips of clouds, and forests mixed sun and shadows to create a spectrum of green that bursts the heart. This was the Oregon I loved. This was the home in which I wanted to both lose myself and be found.

I tried to hold onto Oregon's beauty with each click of my camera, capturing it in stilled images I could keep when we returned home. When Dave and I drove to Mt. St. Helen's, the back of my camera opened as I fumbled to retrieve it out of my bag, exposing the roll of film inside to light. Later, when we would develop the photos from our trip, only the images of the erupted volcano would be affected.

The gutted peak appeared in a shroud of red, as though we had spent the day in the land of nightmares.

Dave and I flew back to New Hampshire without seeing my father, or any of my paternal relatives. They didn't, as far as I knew, know we were in Oregon. Even my grandmother had kept it a secret. Instead, we visited with my maternal relatives who gathered at my grandparents' home for a home-made Italian meal prepared by me and Dave. It was the last supper I would share with Poppy.

Seventeen months later, on December 16, 2001, my beloved grandfather succumbed to acute myelogenous leukemia. The disease took over his compromised body quickly, too quickly for me to react in the way I would later wish I had.

When my mother called me to tell me she was going to Oregon to see her father, I asked her if she wanted me to fly out with her, hoping she would make the decision for me. Hoping and fearing that she would say yes.

"There's no need for you to go. I want to go alone," she told me. So I stayed in New Hampshire.

Two days before Poppy passed, and the day before she flew back to New Hampshire, my mother called me at work so I could say goodbye to my grandfather. I was working in the marketing department of a software company in southern Massachusetts. Although the walls of my cubicle hid my body, it was impossible to hold a private conversation.

"He can barely talk," my mother warned me. "His mouth is full of sores."

Poppy's voice, when my mother put the phone to his mouth, sounded unrecognizable, and I was not prepared to hear all that had already been lost. My heart wanted to hold onto the man who had, despite his arthritis, held me tight while he led me across the dance floor on the day of my wedding. In my mind I held the image of two summers before when we sat together in his kitchen eating bowls of ice cream. I could still see Poppy's unflinching focus as he lifted spoonful upon spoonful of his favorite dessert, a pint in total, coated with milk, until he finally let the metal rest against the empty bowl.

The only words I could hear with certainty from my grandfather's sore-filled mouth were "I love you." Three words that I repeated back, calling him "Poppy" for the last time, through the muffling liquid of tears.

Daughter

deliver me
home

I held in my arms
the memory of nightmares. little girl
grow with
me

strong

In the summer of 2001, Dave and I moved with our cats to a small two-bedroom, one-bathroom ranch-style house in Hudson, New Hampshire. We were more than ready to be away from the grime, congestion and insecurity of Malden, and although we weren't replacing it with the land and privacy we dreamed of, we were thrilled to have a home to call our own.

Our first house wore the decor of the '70s. The shag carpet extended throughout — even in the dining area — in faded reds, blues and whites. The bathroom and kitchen floors were covered in linoleum, and most of the walls were either papered or paneled. We had a lot of work to do, and our families, who were happy to have us back in the state, chipped in to help us.

Tara and I spent a memorable summer day pulling weeds out of the neglected flower gardens, gleefully uncovering paths of rocks and mounds of perennials as our hands made their way to the earth. Inside the house, Dave and my stepfather cut a huge hole in the wall, and hung a picture window we bought for a bargain at a discount building supply store. Our dark living space transformed into a room filled with light as we peeled the faux wood paneling from our walls and rolled primer and white paint.

Dave's father, who owned a furniture store, got us a discount on carpeting, and we tore up the shag, vacuumed out thirty years of collected sand and dirt, and laid down a sea of green throughout most of the house. In the dining and kitchen area, my stepfather supervised Dave as he installed his first wood floor, in pre-finished, 3/4 inch slabs of cherry. For our anniversary, Dave's mother had our bathroom tiled, and the silver disco decor dissolved as we tore down the paper and painted the walls blue. Not a surface in our new home went untouched, and in the photographs we took during those weeks, nearly every member of our two families was captured with paint-brush in hand. When we were finished with our remodeling, our home barely resembled the house we bought.

Our cats were perhaps more thrilled with their new home than we were. After spending the majority of their first years of life inside an apartment, they now had free reign of the outdoors. We cut an oval opening at the bottom of the door leading to our finished basement so Merlin and Tigger could roam the house as they pleased. Another oval was cut into the door leading from our screened porch to the back yard, just in case the cats wanted to take shelter and nap in their "kitty-cups" between hunting excursions. They were living the good life, for a while.

Six months after we moved, Tigger succumbed to a sudden respiratory illness. By the time we brought him to the emergency clinic, it was too late for the veterinarian to save him. Dave and I were devastated by our loss. Before we had our house, we brought our "boys" with us each time we visited New Hampshire so they could explore outdoor living at my parents' home in Canterbury. We spoiled our cats, like only a couple without children can. Tigger had made a habit of climbing our backs to wrap his body around our necks while we walked around the apartment, and later, our house. When we made our lunches in the morning, he would stand on his hind legs and hip-check us until we threw down pieces of turkey. Unless he dug his claws too deep into skin on his way up to our shoulders, he could do no wrong.

When Tigger died, I stayed home from work, and spent the day crying on the couch with Dave and cuddling Merlin. By the time the kids in the neighborhood were making their way home from school, I was tired and angry in my grief. Sitting on the couch, I watched a boy and a girl, about fifteen years of age, flirt in the snowbank beside our driveway.

"Look," I called over to Dave, "They're on our property and they're not moving."

I could hear the couple's laughter through the glass of the window we had installed over the garage. Their happiness fueled my pain, and I hopped off the couch and pushed open one of the side windows.

"Go home," I yelled through the cold, January air, slamming the window shut at their startled expressions.

From my repositioned seat, hidden in the shadows on the sofa, I watched the couple linger for a moment, laughing once again before they slowly made their way out of sight.

A few weeks after Tigger's death, Dave and I adopted an adult cat from a shelter. The decision was easy. Penny, a plump black female with large golden eyes, chose us. When we entered the crowded cat room of the Humane Society, she pushed herself against the door of her cage and telepathically broadcasted her desire to go home with us. "I'm the one for you, pick me," she seemed to be saying while she stared us down with her yellow eyes. As soon as the latch on her cage was free, Penny began sauntering down the hallway to the visiting room. She was all business. How could we refuse?

Merlin and Penny vied for dominance the first few weeks after we brought Penny home. If truth be told, Merlin was a bit of a pest. He was a cat who was out for "number one," and he wasn't about to let this new intruder usurp his position. With time, the two cats learned to share all of the best places to sleep, and peace again settled into our home.

I was now working in marketing, making a good salary and saving money in the anticipation of starting a family. I didn't want to wait the full seven years for Dave to finish both medical school and residency, but I also knew I wouldn't return to work once our first

189

child was born. It was a good job that paid the bills and allowed us to save a bit. What I really wanted, more than anything else, though, was to be a mom.

In the spring of 2003, a couple of months before Dave graduated from medical school, I became pregnant. I fell in love with my first child the moment she moved her tiny hands across my womb, showing me that she was here to stay. I was teased by her touches, which grew stronger each day, making me aware of time. The realization that I would only have this child wholly to myself while she was inside of me, made me want to never release her. For nine months, the love I felt for my developing baby consumed me and made me complete.

Intimately, I knew her. We were, in essence, one body sharing the same breath, the same food, the same blood, and the same thoughts. Three months into my pregnancy my daughter's face appeared to me within the dreams of night. Dave and I had chosen to be surprised by the sex of our first child, but that night I knew I was carrying a girl. In the full detail of a clear photograph, I saw what my daughter would look like six months after she was born.

My daughter's face was a perfect circle, haloed with hair the color of mine. Two enormous eyes, so deeply blue they held no bottoms, appeared above a tiny nose. No words passed from her lips, just those eyes reading the secrets of my soul. *Here I am*, her eyes said. *I am ready for our journey together, are you?* I knew, in that moment, I had been given a great gift. That this child I was carrying inside of me would change my life in ways I could not yet image. In the blue of her eyes I glimpsed a wisdom that had the capacity to fill my heart and break it. I told no one of her visit, but held my secret tucked like a pearl inside the flesh of my womb.

I spoiled my daughter while she grew inside of me, feeding her foods we craved: thick slices of cheese, steak grinders with pickles and more cheese, tuna fish, mint chocolate-chip ice cream, ranch salad dressing, and mashed potatoes. When we were alone, I slipped a maternity yoga tape into the VCR, rolled my blue mat onto the green carpet, and together we saluted the sun through the ceiling. While I folded and stretch, my daughter rolled the walls of my womb, hiccuping happiness.

Our favorite moment was the dance at the end. For the last five minutes of the tape, I would close my eyes to the screen, allowing only the music that sounded like the forest to enter my senses. Inside the canvas of my mind, I painted the green canopy of summer trees above an earthen floor dappled by sunlight. My body swayed with a forest wind as the songs of Earth moved through my bare feet and into my womb. My daughter, in turn, tumbled with the beat. When the yogi's voice would flow over the music, urging all of us women who held babies inside our bellies to imagine a circle of pregnant mothers dancing together, I would imagine a forest where my daughter and I were alone, our own complete circle.

One evening, at the end of autumn, my body began to prepare for the release of my baby. I felt the muscles in my belly squeeze into a fist every five to seven minutes, and started walking the hallway while my husband phoned the hospital to tell them we were on our way. On the phone, Dave inquired about the physician on-call and was told it was Dr. Wood. Dr. Clark, the woman I had chosen for my prenatal care, and who I had hoped would deliver our first child, wasn't due back on the ward until the following week. We'd never met Dr. Wood.

Had we known that our daughter would not arrive until 4:17 a.m. nearly two days later, we might have stayed home a while longer. Instead, we grabbed the bag I had already packed with my bathrobe, a change of clothes, toiletries, snacks and the tiny white pajamas dotted with green and yellow apples. I was still the only one who knew we were having a girl.

At the hospital, I remained in triage while we waited for a bed. At only two centimeters dilated, no one was in a rush but me. Later, when my parents arrived, we still hadn't moved into a private room. After checking to see how I was doing, my stepfather settled into the family waiting area. My mother took her place beside me, preparing to be present for the birth of her first grandchild.

It took a long time. Time that I began to lose track of as I willed my body to dilate fully. When I finally reached eight centimeters, many hours had passed, and my contractions had turned fierce, moving down my womb in an over-whelming need.

"I *need* to push. I *can't* stop it," I told my nurse, who looked at me with the face of practiced concern.

"No, you can't push yet. You have to wait. You need to fight through your contractions," she said.

I thought about women who give birth in fields without western medicine. *Do they*, I wanted to ask, *push against their bodies?* My trust, though, was in the hands of the trained professionals, so I used my dwindling power to fight the will of a body that wanted only to move my child into this world.

When Dr. Wood arrived, he placed his hand inside of me to check the progress of my cervix.

"Can I push?"

My question was met with disappointment, "You still have a lip. Not yet."

His tired voice told me he was discouraged with my body—and with me. I knew I was not meeting his hopes for a quick, easy birth, but he was not the only one who was unhappy. This was not what I had hoped for.

Lying on the hospital bed, fighting contractions, I felt weak, exhausted, and defeated. Still, I wasn't ready to give up. I dug into my reserves of energy so I could continue to wage a battle against my body. As each wave crested inside of me, I clamped my jaw, and willed my muscles to stop their desire to push. My body's protests broke free in loud cries, unearthed from deep within me. The "No" my voice released was dark, primal, and drawn-out to the length of each agonizing contraction.

The fight against my body continued for two more hours, until I became so exhausted I was ready to concede defeat. According to Dr. Wood, who turned his head to me with resignation after he again checked my cervix, the lip was still there, so I accepted his offer of an epidural. I already felt I had failed at my first attempt at childbirth.

When the fluid pumping into my spine from the epidural entered my bloodstream, I relaxed. Too much. I no longer felt exhausted. I no longer felt my body's desire to push. Instead, I was content to wait out the long hours ahead, and began chatting in my bed to my mother and Dave, like I was thirteen staying up all night with my friends. More than twenty hours had passed since I first stepped inside the hospital doors, and as I looked at the nodding heads of my mother and husband, who had both stayed awake with me, I realized this was far from a slumber party.

An hour later, Dr. Wood popped in for another cervix check. "Turn down the epidural," he told my nurse. "It's stalling the birth."

By his next visit, the lip that had lingered for so long had finally disappeared.

"It's time to push," Dr. Wood spoke the words I had been waiting to hear.

I pushed hard, or so I thought, again and again as Dr. Wood impatiently waited for a sign of my daughter's head.

"You need to try harder," the words sounded like a reprimand. "You're not pushing effectively."

My lower body was still numb, and the intensity of the waves that came through me before the drug had entered my spine were weakened. I felt like I was pushing against a soft sponge. There was nothing for me to register my body's ability to successfully bring my daughter into the world. Instead, my only choice was to rely upon Dr. Wood, whose frustration grew, as he told me again that I was not doing enough.

Slowly, the drugs from the epidural faded and were replaced by the over-whelming feeling of exhaustion and defeat. When I tried pushing again, there were no reserves of strength to draw upon. Frustrated, Dr. Wood began talking about forceps. A word that made me seize in panic.

I gathered all of my remaining reserves of energy, determined to birth my baby without help as Dr. Wood felt for the top of my daughter's head, which remained firmly stuck. It wasn't enough.

"It's time for forceps," he told the nurse.

I looked to my husband who was in his first year of residency for family practice medicine, to my mother, a nurse practitioner of women's health, and to the nurse who had stuck by my side. Through the fog of exhaustion, I heard my husband mention the possibility of a c-section or a vacuum, followed by Dr. Wood's insistence that forceps were our best option.

After he left the room to prep, my nurse assured me, "Don't worry. Dr. Wood is very skilled with forceps deliveries."

What kind of doctor specializes in forceps?! I wanted to ask.

For the remainder of my daughter's birth, I entered a world that seemed to spiral into the distant past, where pain came second only to death. When the only choice for a difficult birth was to reach into a woman's womb and pull with the cold, hard hands of metal.

194

When Dr. Wood pushed the forceps inside of me, I felt the walls of my vagina tense into shock. The feeling of violation, of my body being stretched and torn, was so intense and sudden my mouth released a scream that would not stop until the moment my daughter was pulled out of me. The vibration of my voice reached its desperate energy through the walls of the small room and sent its echoed haunt down the hallway. I saw the shadow of my pain frozen on the faces of my mother and husband, who could do nothing but hold my hands.

Although the trauma of my daughter's birth haunted my body and mind long after she was pulled into the world, the moment I held her in my arms I pushed the nightmare aside and focused on her light. While I studied the little girl formed from the silky strands of her parents' DNA, grown into a solid baby with the nutrients from her mother's body, I relaxed into the realization that she was mostly unharmed. Aside from the hematoma forming a cone of bruised tissue on the top of her head, my daughter was perfect. We named her Ava.

As I studied my daughter, I marveled at her brazen curiosity. Her eyes assessing her surroundings told me she was more than ready to take on her new world. With reluctance I let her go for the first time, passing her into the arms of her father, and then my mother. Ava, in turn, held her head high without support and took in the new world around her.

On Christmas day, I bathed and buttoned Ava into a red-and-white knitted onesie, with a picture of Santa Claus on her chest. I tied booties onto her tiny feet and pulled a matching hat over the peak of her head. Even after three weeks, my daughter wore the hematoma of her birth.

Dave, Ava and I stayed home to celebrate our first Christmas together. In the afternoon, relatives we had invited to stop by began to arrive. My mother and stepfather were followed by my sister and her husband, who were expecting their first child in spring. Later, Dave's side of the family appeared bearing more gifts. Each person took a turn holding our daughter, who grew sleepy from the stimulation. As the darkness of night began to show through the window behind her, Ava fell asleep on the soft chest of my husband's cousin, and while I watched my daughter's peaceful slumber, the hollow in my belly began to ache.

I was used to having my daughter all to myself. Dave worked long hours as a resident, and Ava and I would spend our days, and many nights, alone with the cats. Ava absorbed everything around her. Her eyes were like two blue wells without bottoms. The world before her tumbled into their depths, and she held onto its magic. She resisted sleep, and fought the closing of her lids.

We had a treadmill in our basement, and many a night Dave or I (usually Dave if he was home), would strap Ava onto the front of one of our chests and walk her. At two-thirty in the morning our tired legs would try to lull our daughter to sleep.

Sometimes, during the day, Ava and I would dance. When I thought it was time for her to nap, I put Nora Jones on the CD player in an attempt to hypnotize my daughter's busy mind and body into rest.

Eventually she caught on, and the instant Nora's husky lyrics began to beat their way out of the speakers, Ava would cry and wriggle her body in protest against my arms.

Ava was not an easy baby. She tested her parents' limits of endurance, as she did during her delivery, and as she does while she grows. A wise, old soul, she is, in many ways, our teacher. The love that bound the three of us together is intensely rooted through many lifetimes. Ava, though, was also a soft baby. When she would nurse she would succumb to my mother-love, letting it fill her belly while her tiny hands twirled my hair into ropes.

Eight months after Ava's birth, I missed my period. For two weeks I was in denial, telling myself my hormones were seeking balance. One day, while my husband was at work, I dug through the bathroom cabinet and found what I was looking for.

I took the pregnancy test already knowing what the result would be, but hoping I was wrong. It wasn't that I didn't want another baby, I just didn't want one so soon. Dave had always talked about having as many as three kids, while I wanted two. Either way, we agreed, we were planning on spacing them out by at least two years.

We had not been careful, relying on a sporadic use of a diaphragm and the fact that I was breast-feeding to minimize our risk of pregnancy. Our second child, we would later do the math, was conceived on our five-year wedding anniversary.

I spent the rest of the day, after I took the pregnancy test, crying and holding Ava. At that moment, she was the only baby I wanted. The only baby I could conceive of giving my love to. My pregnancy made me feel as though I had betrayed my daughter. She would, I mourned with guilt, only have me wholly to herself for less than a year and a half. Ava wouldn't remember being an only child. It took me many months to see the blessings in this truth.

I was also afraid. Haunting me was the specter of my daughter's birth, and the fear that I might have to relive its horror. I spent more time silently fearing the birth of my second child than I did trying to get to know the baby rapidly growing inside my womb.

The pregnancy was easy. I never had the early months of nausea that I did with Ava, and my body had the ability to accept any nutrients I gave it. Perhaps because I was nursing through most of my pregnancy, I also gained less weight, and even in the last few months, I experienced no swelling of ankles or fingers.

197

There were moments when I could almost convince myself that I wasn't pregnant, but these were fleeting. When Ava wanted to nurse, I would lie her growing body against the swelling mound of her sibling's, and wonder if both of my children were getting what they needed from their mother; if there was enough of me to evenly divide.

Despite my guilt for having gotten pregnant so soon after my daughter's birth, I wanted to fall in love with my developing baby. It had been so easy to fall in love with Ava before her birth. Unlike with our first pregnancy, my husband and I decided to find out the sex of the fetus during a routine ultrasound. I hoped this knowledge would help me bond with a baby I felt was coming too soon.

Dave was overjoyed with the finger-like projection that appeared on the screen between the fetus's legs during the ultrasound. He loved his daughter without bounds, but I knew he had been hoping for a son for our second child. With some surprise, I realized I had been too.

Still, I focused on my daughter. I wanted to give her all of the undivided attention I knew she would miss once her brother was born. I wanted to hold her always in my arms, knowing that soon they would be filled with another form. I didn't want to see how quickly she was moving towards her independence. Ava was, I would later realize, much more prepared and ready to have a baby brother than I was to have a second child.

Nine months passed quickly. The night before my due date, I crawled into bed with a feeling of unease. My body, I knew, was preparing for the birth of my son, but my mind was still not ready. I willed myself back into sleep, waking each hour to the warnings of my womb, which I pushed aside and covered with restless slumber until five o'clock in the morning when I nudged my husband.

"I think we should go to the hospital," I told him. "But don't wake Ava yet."

Dave checked my cervix to be sure.

"You're about five centimeters," he said. "We should get going."

We let our daughter sleep until we were ready to get in the car. Dave and I decided early in the pregnancy that we would not return to the hospital of my daughter's birth. There was no way I was going to risk a repeat of the experience I had with my first delivery. Instead, we chose a facility physician at the hospital where Dave was completing his residency. Dr. Benson assured us that she would be at the birth of our second child, and she was.

After we buckled Ava into her car-seat to begin the forty minute drive north to the hospital, Dave called Dr. Benson to let her know we were on our way. She was just finishing an early morning run. "You couldn't have timed it better," she told him. "I'll shower and be right in."

We timed my contractions as we drove, and I breathed through them in silence every five minutes. My mind was focused on my daughter in the backseat, and I turned around to study her beautiful face between the pulls of my belly to check for signs of unease. Always she appeared happy, our sixteen-and-a-half-month-old little girl, chatting and smiling up at us as though this was just another car ride to Gammy and Gampy's.

My parents were walking towards the entrance of the hospital when my husband pulled up to the curb at six o'clock in the morning. They followed us inside, trying to take Ava into their arms so my husband could help me walk. My daughter, sensing the urgency of her surroundings, wrapped her own arms tight around my legs. I knew she wanted me to bend down and lift her, but I couldn't. My strength was focused on my belly, my arms circling the little boy whose body was pushing with a quiet intensity towards the earth.

"Please, take Ava," I begged my parents, unable to look into my daughter's face.

My mother unwound Ava from my legs, and scooped her into her arms as we went through the hospital doors. Once inside, Ava achieved her freedom, and quickly found her way again to my legs. I was now standing in triage, waiting for Dr. Benson to arrive. Having my daughter clinging to me with her need was too much to bear. My little girl, already, had seen too much.

"Please take her home," I told my parents through breath I was struggling to control.

Over-whelmed by the pain of guilt, I couldn't watch my daughter leave or think about the fact that she would not be with me for the next two days. We had never yet been apart, and Ava seemed to know what was coming. "She'll be okay," my mother assured me with a smile. "We'll take good care of her. This is for the best." I tried to believe her.

Moments later my doctor arrived pulling on her lab coat and grabbing gloves from the box on the wall as she peered at my hunched body.

"Do you want to try to lie down on the bed?" she asked. "So I can check your cervix?"

"No," I told her, unable to move. "No, I think I need to stay standing."

Dr. Benson kneeled to reach under my hospital gown. When she removed her hand she looked surprised.

"You're fully dilated," she told me. "Are you ready to start pushing?"

If I could have conversed with my body at that moment, it would have told me how it had labored silently through the night and the long car ride. It would have told me that it could not wait much longer to release a little boy ready to come into the world. Instead, I was waiting to feel the pain I believed would arrive at any moment with the force of a hurricane. It would not be until later, after my son was born and in my arms, that I would view my body with awe for working in silence through the night, for dilating five centimeters during a forty minute drive, and for waiting until my daughter was safely out of sight to release a sound of labor.

After Dr. Benson told me I was ready for delivery, she asked if I wanted a birthing stool. It was an option we had previously discussed, and I nodded my head. The thought of giving birth with gravity on my side appealed to me. Once again, I let my mind fill with images of women in fields and forests, laboring alone to birth their children. I thought of their strength and their courage, and for the first time since my daughter's birth, I thought maybe it was in me too.

When the stool arrived, its metal frame looked small and inadequate. As I eased my body around it, I felt vulnerable.

"Can you support my back?" I asked Dave.

With my husband bracing me, I gripped the metal arms of the stool. I immediately felt an over-whelming need to push.

"I can't do this," I told my doctor. "I think I need something. Can I have something?" My voice wore my growing panic.

Dr. Benson smiled an infuriatingly knowing smile. "You'll be fine, Alethea. You can do this."

She was right. With the first push, the power of my body collected into each muscle fiber as they came together to seize upon the task of birthing my son. I became acutely aware of the strength of my sex. I knew, in that moment, I would birth my child without help, and I pushed through the pain that was now burning in a satisfying sear across my stretching flesh.

"His head is crowning, do you want to feel it?" Dr. Benson asked after my second push.

I freed one hand from its grip on the stool, leaning against my husband, as I reached my fingers down to touch the wet silk of my son's hair. One more time, I grabbed the metal bars of the stool, and the muscles of my body seized into a final push to release my second child.

As my son slid out of my body, the cry that sang through my mouth was the cry of joy, of strength, and of gratitude for this little boy who came so easily into my life. I held my son to my breast, urging his lips to find the new source of his food, and hugged the full weight of his body against mine. In that moment I knew I'd never want to let him go. With my son in my arms I found the fullness of my love. A love that was always present, waiting to be given.

Voice

I want to
birth

words

articulate need, the depth of emotion
unearth them waiting
deep inside I see a girl
seeking light

When I was pregnant with our son Alex, Dave and I began planning for an addition on our house. We wanted our children to be able to have their own rooms, so we asked my stepfather to lead the construction of an energy efficient addition. Since we were still strapped for cash, my stepfather offered to settle up on his labor costs after he finished with his portion of the project. Before he helped us with our additional, though, my stepfather had built a garage for my sister and her husband, and charged them the full cost of his labor, plus materials. My sister, understandably, was not happy when she found out about our verbal agreement.

My stepfather traveled to our home with his equipment when he was not working elsewhere, to get the foundation poured and the walls raised and framed. To show our gratitude, and to help compensate him for his work, Dave and I purchased several gifts for my stepfather over the next several months, including tools, a recliner chair, and a new TV. We also treated him and my mother to a weekend at the Balsams with us. Later, when he decided it was time to settle up on what we owed him, my stepfather suggested we write him a check for several thousand dollars, and he would give half of it to my sister. "To make it even," he said.

I'm not sure anyone was happy with this arrangement. My stepfather believed we were to be treated like paying customers, and Tara and I felt we had been served another dose of his conditional love. "Aren't parents supposed to give freely?" my sister and I asked each other, comparing our lives to those of our friends. I personally knew of a friend whose father insisted upon building her entire house free of charge, no strings attached. His only condition was that he wanted his daughter to "have her dream home." Tara and I both had friends whose parents took their young families to Disney and on cruises, while Dave and I had taken my parents to the Balsams Grand Resort as another way to say "thank you" for my stepfa-

205

ther's work. We felt we were always in his debt, while other parents we knew relished the opportunity to give freely and unconditionally to their children and grandchildren.

It took Dave and me awhile to complete our addition after my stepfather did his part. We hired out the plumbing and heating, but while our children slept, we mudded, painted and put down a cork floor in the basement and a bamboo floor upstairs in our new bedroom. The addition was finished just in time, as my husband likes to joke, to put our house on the market, a year and half after Alex's birth.

I was, with the support of my family who wanted us to move closer, pushing for us to move. In my mind, there was little reason to be living in Hudson. Dave had accepted a position as a family practice physician in Hooksett, NH, and as a stay-at-home-mom with few friends with kids nearby, I was lonely. Eventually I convinced Dave we would be happier in a smaller, less congested town with a good school system that was closer to our families and Dave's job. Even though he wasn't eager to leave behind all of the hard work we had put into our home, Dave agreed to the move.

It took a year to sell our house. A year that brought with it more than the challenges of trying to sell a home with two little kids who still needed naps, and were not worried about being neat and tidy. In the fall of 2005, a few months before we put our house on the market, our cat Merlin developed a lump on his side. The mass grew within two months to the size of a clementine. We brought Merlin to the vets and had the lump biopsied. The results were discouraging, but we went ahead and had surgery to remove it, knowing there was a good chance of it growing back. Within a couple of weeks, another lump started to form. Briefly, we debated the option of chemotherapy, but decided not to put our beloved pet through the discomfort.

Instead, we tried to make Merlin's last months of life as comfortable as possible.

While Merlin was ill, our house became infested with fleas. First we noticed a few black specks on our couch, then the kids started getting bites. Fleas propagate quickly, and soon they were bouncing off the green carpet of our living room when we walked through the house. We applied Frontline to the cats and washed bedding and cushion covers. We vacuumed daily. Still the fleas persisted. We went to the pet store, where we were told our only option was to bomb our house with chemicals. So I started searching the internet for natural remedies. I went to battle with boxes of Borax, pouring the white powder over the carpet at night like flakes of fake snow. In the morning, I vacuumed up the powder with the desiccated bodies of fleas.

When we decided it was time to let Merlin pass, we called our veterinary office, hoping they would grant our wish for a home euthanization. They would not oblige, so we asked Dave's cousin, a young veterinarian, who offered to drive over the next morning to put Merlin to sleep.

We let our children, who were both too young to fully understand death, say their goodbyes before we shut the door to the porch where Merlin was resting in his kitty cup. While Dave's cousin talked us through the two shots she was about to administer, we stroked our cat's fur. Merlin, who seemed to accept fully our love and his fate, looked into our eyes and purred until he peacefully passed.

Ava was old enough to mourn Merlin. In an attempt to assuage her grief and ours, we got her a kitten. Olivia, an orange tabby, arrived in a box delivered by a friend a few weeks after Merlin's death. The bond between the kitten and her two-and-half-year-old mommy developed quickly. Ava toted Olivia around the house much like the storybook pig she was named for totes around her cat Edwin, holding her under the arms like a rag doll. Olivia, the cat, never scratched, and relished every display of affection bestowed upon her by her favorite human.

Although we had an adorable new family member to divert our attention away from the loss of Merlin, life continued to challenge us. While Dave was a medical student, he had enrolled in a program with the National Guard that promised him $50,000 in medical school loan repayments in return for one weekend of drill a month, plus two weeks of service a year at a local guard base. Dave dutifully carried out his National Guard obligations until a few months before Alex's birth when his commanders told him the $50,000 loan repayment had been stripped from the program. He would never see the money. This broken promise, along with the birth of our second child, led to our decision for Dave to leave the military. The National Guard, though, didn't want to let him go.

The first letters to arrive from his commanders stated that Dave was obligated to serve eight years — and not the agreed upon six — before he could request an honorable discharge. Weeks passed, and then copies of contracts, forged with a signature that didn't match my husband's, arrived in our mail. We knew we were in trouble. A few weeks after Dave graduated from residency, and two months after we put our house on the market, the first set of deployment orders came.

We hired one of the most prominent lawyers in the state, and a handwriting specialist. It took several months, and thousands of dollars we could hardly afford, to verify that my husband's signature had not been written with his hand. My husband contacted our state senators and representatives, as well as the governor, several of whom, including the governor, wrote letters on his behalf. Still, the letters from the military kept coming. The dates of deployment moved up with each one. It didn't seem to matter that a specialist had verified the forgery of my husband's signature on the contract, or that Dave had saved emails from recruiters stating that he would "never face deployment," and could "get out at any time," because the deployment orders continued to arrive.

Three months after my husband received his first deployment letter, and a month after my daughter started preschool, I woke in the middle of the night with stomach pains so intense they rivaled active labor. It took three hours for my intestines to move the food they were struggling to process out of my body. During those hours, it was impossible to find the sanctuary of sleep, so I stationed myself in a mound of misery beside the toilet. I had no idea what was happening to me; I only knew my body had lost control over its balance.

This loss of balance extended to my emotions, which now seemed to boil over with little provocation. I was having a hard time keeping it together. Seemingly little incidents would easily magnify into omens of disaster inside of my mind.

One day, before a showing of our home, I dusted the living room. While I worked, Alex played happily with a pile of blocks in the filtered sunshine on the carpet. Ava, ever restless, was bouncing on the cushions of the couch.

"Be careful," I warned, watching her from the corner of my eye.

I swiped the cloth across the cherry wood of the bookshelf, willing the dust to disappear. Making my way to the top, I lifted knickknacks as I balanced on the edge of the same couch my daughter was using as a trampoline. My eyes were focused on the dust when I felt the release of Ava's weight, followed by the dull thud of her body hitting the carpet. There was a brief pause, then another, smaller, thud.

I looked down from my perch to make sure my daughter was okay from her short jump. Beside Ava I saw the broken pieces of gray stone on the carpet. The Shona Family of Four figurine my husband had given me for Christmas was knocked off its precarious perch on a speaker by Ava during her fall, and lay shattered into five pieces on the floor.

"Ava, look what you've done!" I shouted in a voice trembling with an anger that exceeded the magnitude of the accident. My eyes were fixed on the broken family scattered across the floor.

"I'm sorry," Ava replied, following my gaze to the pieces of gray stone beside us.

My daughter's matter-of-fact apology fueled my emotions.

"You've ruined it!" I cried out. "Look what you've done!"

Hot tears were now boiling out of my eyes. "You *need* to be more careful! You've ruined Daddy's gift to Mommy," I added.

I needed my young daughter to feel my pain. I needed her to see the magnitude of what she had so carelessly done.

Fear began to spread wide my daughter's eyes, and I watched as my beautiful little girl turned to look again at the mess on the floor.

"I'm sorry," she repeated. "Daddy can glue it when he gets home. He'll fix it," she added with assurance.

I found little comfort in my daughter's confident words. In her world, mending the broken was as simple as having her daddy apply adhesive. Ava, I knew, because we had chosen not to tell her, had no idea that her father could be sent away at any moment. She had no fear that our family might be ripped apart in a manner that could never be mended. She only knew that her mother was devastated by a broken statue.

"I don't think so," I told Ava, as my love for her slowly folded the edges of my fear. With her help, I began to pick the fragments from the floor.

Later that night, as my daughter had promised, my husband gathered the broken gray bodies and glued them back together. The next morning, I placed the repaired statue high on the bookshelf while my eyes searched for cracks in the stone.

Months passed with relative peace, until one spring night I went to bed with a feeling of unease that was more than the usual anxiety I got when my husband was on call and I was left alone in the house with my two young children. My daughter's cat, Olivia, had refused to come inside for the night, and I was worried. It wasn't the first time she had chosen not to appear when I called for her, but we always tried our best to get our cats in a night.

Several times before I went to bed, I called for Olivia. Finally, giving up around midnight, I shut the door to the porch for the last time, reassuring myself that Dave would probably be home soon, see the note I had left him, and let Olivia inside.

At 4:00 a.m., two hours before Dave arrived home, I woke suddenly. Seconds later, I heard the scream. Instinctively I knew I had been pulled from sleep in time to witness my daughter's beloved pet's last cry for life. I also knew, before I got my body to the door and met the silence that took over the night, that I was too late to save her. Olivia's final cry would haunt me for years.

Even though I knew in my heart it was futile, I stepped out into the darkness to call for Olivia. I searched the ground for evidence, but saw no sign of life, or death. Reluctantly, I returned to my bed. For the remainder of the night I fought with sleep, knowing I would need it to help get me through the day ahead. In the long hours before dawn, my restless mind played with guilt and grief. *What was I going to tell my daughter?*

When Ava woke, she looked for her beloved pet, as she did each morning.

"Where is Olivia?" she asked.

I turned away, trying to shield her from the sorrow behind my eyes.

211

"She's not here. I think she's gone," I added quietly.

"When will she be back?"

"I don't think she's coming back, sweetie," I said as I tried to draw Ava into an embrace.

"Maybe she just ran away," Ava said as she pulled against me. "We should go look for her."

My daughter was focused on finding her pet, but I couldn't participate in her futile search. I knew with an unexplainable certainty that Olivia was gone. More than anything, I wanted to take back the night and find Ava's beloved cat before she succumbed to her tragic fate, but my only choice was to find a way to soften the inevitable news.

I couldn't lie to my daughter. I didn't want to give her false hope, but I also couldn't tell her why I knew Olivia was not coming home. In my mind I saw a circle of coyotes on the lawn. I saw an orange cat fleeing for the safety of the porch.

"Maybe she just ran away," Ava offered. "We should put up signs because someone might find her."

"Maybe," I said. "But I don't think so, honey. I don't think she's coming home."

I let Ava hold out hope for a few days that Olivia might return. I struggled with her grief, and my own, laden with guilt. We never put up signs, and one day, when I was ready, I told her why.

A few months after we lost Olivia, we got a new kitten, which Ava hand-selected from a litter in Canterbury. She named her new pet Yoda after the Star Wars character she adored. The lovable tiger-striped tabby is still with us today.

In the middle of October of 2007, we moved Yoda and Penny with us to our new home in Bow, NH. We were now just across town from my sister and her family. Twenty minutes from my parents, and twenty minutes from Dave's. I was convinced life would become easier, and better for us.

My body and emotions, though, continued in their struggled for peace. For seven more months, I tried in vain to digest my turmoil while I fought sleep at night. Until, one day, I decided it had to end.

I am awake to read the red glow of the clock beside my husband's side of the bed: 3:15 a.m. It's a typical time for my stomach to wake me, and I sigh with resignation. The plate of pasta I consumed for dinner is now churning with the half-glass of red wine I had with it. There is too much acid in my belly, and I know I am not going to make it peacefully through the rest of the night.

I try my first line of defense, rolling over onto my belly in an attempt to muffle its pains. In a matter of minutes, I am clenching my legs to my chest, curled up on my side. *Not today,* I plead with my body. *It's Mother's Day.*

My body, way past the stage of reason, is focused only on its efforts to release the remnants of my dinner. It feels like there's a volcano inside of me. The lava is burning away my insides. Its sulfuric breath bloating as it searches for air.

I glance once more at the clock. The red lights flash 3:30 a.m. as I ease my body off the side of the bed, hoping I won't wake Dave on my way to our bathroom. My bloated belly is clutched in my hands as though I am cradling a fetus ready to be released.

In five steps, I reach the bathroom, and the hard, cold surface of the tile sends needles through the soles of my feet. I will not be warm again for ninety minutes. Resigned to this routine, I pull the bathmat off the top of the shower, and spread it beside the bowl of the toilet. I think of the warm wrap of my bathrobe, hanging in my closet, but can't muster the effort required to retrieve it. Below the sink there is a bottle of white calcium carbonate discs, and packages of Omeprazole tablets. I know from two years of dealing with these

213

episodes, two to three times a week, that these pills have no chance of easing the pain in my abdomen. My only choice is to count down the long minutes, while I struggle to find a position of relative comfort on the damp surface of the bathmat.

An hour passes, and the cramping in my belly begins to descend into my intestines. I breathe a small sigh of relief, knowing that within the next half-hour I will finally find release.

At 5:00 a.m., after the unwanted contents of my stomach have been expelled into the bowl of the toilet, I creep my exhausted body back into the warmth of my bed to retrieve whatever sleep will grant me, while the indigo dawn turns to gray.

In the many months leading up to that fateful Mother's Day of 2008, I searched for the magic pill that would put me back to normal. When I first told my mother and primary care physician about my stomach condition, they both suggested the possibility of IBS. To me IBS sounded mortifying and embarrassing. There was also, as I discovered through internet research, no real medical cure. No, I decided, I couldn't have IBS. I latched onto other possibilities mentioned by my doctor. I agreed to try prescription-strength antacids, and have the blood tests for peptic ulcers and celiac disease.

The pills didn't really help, and the blood tests turned up negative. In January of 2008 my husband and I went to see a specialist, who put a camera attached to a tube down my throat. Before the endoscopy I sat in the prep room with Dave, shivering in my hospital gown with white blankets piled around my legs.

When I was called into the procedure room, the gastroenterologist prepped me by describing the process of easing the tube down my throat. He also told me there was a good possibility I would involuntarily gag. The medicine I had taken, he explained, would erase any memory of this discomfort. I found the idea of an erased memory of an event that sounded like torture, more horrifying than comforting. I felt helpless, like I did when my daughter was born, with the prospect of another foreign object violating my body. There was no turning back, though. I wanted answers.

The medication to erase memory did its job. When my awareness returned to me, I heard the voice of my doctor telling me I had done fine, and that although my body had initially protested the invasion of the tube, he had been able to get a clear view down to my stomach. He had seen some inflammation, he told me, but there were no signs of an ulcer or anything else abnormal.

With the diagnosis of "unexplainable inflammation," we seemed to be frustratingly back to where we had started. The episodes continued making their appearances in the middle of the night. If I had them three or four times in one week, my body would sometimes become too exhausted to care for my children on my own. On these occasions, I would have to ask my husband or my mother to take a sick day from work to help me. I hated having to do this. I hated living with a body out of control. Most of all, I hated not being able to care for my own children.

I began that Mother's Day of 2008 exhausted after my night of unrest. After a lunch at home, the four of us headed into Manchester to see the New Hampshire Fisher Cats play baseball from a VIP balcony reserved by my brother-in-law, a local sports' reporter. At the game, we met up with my sister's family of four, my parents, and my brother-in-law's family. I don't particularly enjoy watching baseball, but I agreed to the game because everyone else seemed delighted by the idea of spending Mother's Day afternoon at the ballpark.

The air outside the closed-in section of the balcony box was chilly and windy. The sky stayed stubbornly overcast. When the lobster rolls my stepfather and daughter so eagerly awaited arrived, I nibbled one, wondering as I did, how my stomach would respond. Normally, I relished the opportunity to eat lobster.

After we ate, I moved outside to watch the game with my family, hugging my coat against the chill. My children took breaks playing with their cousins to vie for my lap. As I lifted first one child, and then another, onto my exhausted body, I made a vow not to let them spend another moment worrying about whether their mother would have enough energy to get them through another day.

The next morning, I went to see my primary care physician. While I sat in the exam room, I told her I could not continue living like this. I agreed to see the specialist one more time, and before I left my doctor handed me a prescription for Bentyl, a jar of small dark blue pills I would fill, but never swallow. "Just in case you have another episode at night," she told me. I had finally started to accept the frustratingly vague diagnosis of IBS.

On May 27, my husband and I drove to Bedford, N.H. to meet with the gastroenterologist. "You know," he said, "I've been telling a lot of my patients who have your types of symptoms to increase their intakes of true fibers. You can start by eating a high fiber cereal before you go to bed." "I know it sounds simple," he added, "but you might want give it a try." I was already eating a healthy fiber-rich diet, but a bowl of cereal a night sounded better than any of the other options presented to me in the past.

"What about probiotics?" I asked, remembering a suggestion made by my mother-in-law.

"Why not," he said, "A lot of my patients have been trying those as well. It can't hurt."

I left the specialist's office armed with a plan that promised relief without medication. My nightly episodes became a nightmare of the past, but I still had more pain to unearth before a more steady-state of balance would prevail in my daily life.

For the next three months I managed to maintain a relatively steady state of balance. Then I turned thirty-five.

I begin my birthday hurling miniature boulders I find half-buried beneath the leaves in the woods, throwing them onto the lawn. It's what I need to do as I battle the turmoil inside of my mind.

I pull each imperfect form, heavy with the weight of gray density, away from beds of detritus. I brush aside their blankets of brown decay, and carry my rocks, one at a time, over to the red maple where I am forming a circle around the tree. Later, I will fill the ground with irises my mother has given me in an old sheetrock bucket of my stepfather's. The irises were pulled and divided from their garden in Canterbury, where each June they grew big and beautiful in their beds of manure.

I need to bring more rocks out of the woods, and I need to rip the grass from the earth around my chosen tree. Mixing the green into brown, I pull it out in lumps, only to give it to the woods in exchange for rocks. I have no use for these soft green spikes, and their roots that stretch and twine into mazes. The hidden matrices hold each individual blade to its neighbors, forming a tangled network that stays together when I pull.

I need rocks, with edges that overlap like puzzle pieces, hiding gaps. With each stone, I rework form, striving for a perfect circle with a diameter of at least twelve feet. My mother has given me a lot of bulbs, and I have lilies to plant as well, to fill the spaces between the irises.

Today, on my thirty-fifth birthday, I need to throw. I need to dig. I need to plant new life into this Earth that I love. Its healing body lets me dig with metal and bare fingers into its flesh and discard what I don't want as long as I give it something back in return; something green with roots to replace what I have removed.

While I dig and plant, I try not to look at the two children who are running confused circles through the yard with their anxious father. He keeps them busy by chasing them away from the stones I hurl out of the woods. As they pass, they pause to look at their mother who waters the soil with a raging sorrow they don't understand, but fear.

The three-year-old boy does not yet know how much he reminds his mother of her child-self. That if you took a photo from each, at the same age, and placed them side-by-side, you would not know how to tell them apart. The five-year-old girl who runs with the little boy across the yard cannot yet understand why there's a storm inside the woman who birthed her, and whose love for her has over-powered and consumed her since she rocked with the waves in her belly. The same waves still crash inside of her mother, their force building until they push against the walls of her skin, spilling their waters out of her eyes. They blur her path to the little girl she could have been. This daughter is starting to understand in a way she shouldn't, her mother's turmoil. She knows enough to give her space.

My circle garden, I realized after two hours of digging earth and placing stones, would not be complete in one day. The labor was enough to tire me so that I no longer wept or felt the urge to pull and throw. When the fire inside of me had died down, I left my unfinished project and went inside to find my children and husband reading books together on the sofa. Three faces greeted my entrance with nervous love, and guilt settled into my body, covered over with brown stains of soil and grass. On my way to shower, I stopped and kissed the tops my children's heads. Although he did not deserve my resentment, I was upset with my husband for planning a birthday dinner with my parents without my consent. He was, in defense, just following a long family tradition.

Later, I found a moment alone with Dave while our children were playing.

"I don't want my parents to come over for dinner," I confessed.

"What do you want me to do?" he asked. "They're probably already on their way over."

I had no choice but to pick up the phone and call them.

My mother answered with a voice soft and sweet. "Happy birthday, honey," she told me. "We were just about to leave."

"I had a tough day," I confessed a partial truth. "I'm not sure I want to have a birthday dinner tonight."

There was a pause, and I knew my mother was processing my words, trying as best she could, to read the message underneath. "Why don't we come over and you and Dave can go out to dinner alone instead?" she offered. I knew they were counting on seeing their grandchildren.

Her words did not bring the outcome I wanted. At that moment, I was unable to articulate my needs, or to comprehend the depth and source of my emotions. I had only just begun to unearth a long buried and complex network of pain. My mother, though, was waiting for my answer. So I accepted her offer, and somewhere deep inside of me, I saw the shadow of a girl seeking light.

Four months pass. My garden of irises and lilies is now sleeping under a thick blanket of snow. We've just had another storm, and instead of rocks, I'm hurling snow. Shovelfuls of the heavy wet stuff. I scoop and heave, scoop and heave as my children glide their kid-sized shovels across the exposed pavement, pretending to help. We've been out here for forty-five minutes, and we're all starting to get crabby and cold, but the driveway isn't finished and I won't stop until it is. Technically, I only need to clear a small space at the end so my husband can park his car safely off the road after work, and then later after he's eaten and the kids are in bed, he'll clear the rest of the snow. Even though Dave doesn't mind shoveling, I don't want to leave the task I've started unfinished. Somewhere in the back of my mind I hear my stepfather's words, *A job worth doing, is worth doing right.*

I'm tired, and the sweat dripping down my back is mixing with the icy flakes of snow that sneak past the collar of my jacket. Nearby, my three-year-old son and five-year-old daughter are no longer happily shoveling tiny scoops of snow but each other into the expanding banks beside the driveway.

"Leave each other alone!" I yell between shovelfuls.

My children ignore me, continuing their battle in the snow.

"Go inside and watch TV! I'll be done in ten minutes," I tell them.

Now that I've released my children from their misery and the cold, I worry about the snow they are tracking through the house, and whether they've managed to remove their wet clothes by themselves. I worry if they're getting along again, or if they are now fighting about whether to watch "Thomas the Tank Engine" (my son) or "Cyberchase" (my daughter, who will inevitably win because she's older, bigger, and bossier).

With my children inside, I realize how much I don't want to be out here shoveling this fucking snow. I'd rather be inside curled up on the couch with my kids, but I can't stop. I have to finish, even though my left shoulder is going numb, my biceps are about to give out, and my body is experiencing that uncomfortable mix of hot and cold.

As I fling the last six feet of accumulated flakes in front of the garage, Ann appears. She's not literally here of course. I haven't seen Ann since I ran into her at L.L.Bean when we were in our early twenties. That last awkward encounter when we both pretended we were old childhood friends. Now, as I shovel the final clumps of snow from the driveway I realize I am angry. That all of that buried hurt I endured when we were teenagers has caused me to feel this sudden, boiling of rage. The emotion of revenge is fleeting, but intense. The snow I am shoveling takes the form of Ann's body, and I dig the blade one final time into its white surface, flinging its heavy bulk over the bank. My heart slows as I put the shovel away and close the door to the garage, but my mind is reminding me that I'm still waiting for Ann to say "I'm sorry."

Four weeks pass, and I am now sitting in the Oak Room of the Manor House at Goddard College. The walls around me are paneled in dark, chiseled mahogany. Pewter sconces balance the ends of a gray, stone fireplace. An old piano is pushed off to the side. The same piano that is sometimes played, rumor has it, by an apparition of a mother clothed in a long black dress as she sits beside the ghost of her young daughter.

Tonight I'm not here to see ghosts, at least not the piano player and her daughter. Instead, I'm sitting with about forty other graduate students, and a handful of faculty, in a circle around the perimeter of the room. We're waiting, anxiously, for Peter, the director of the MFA in creative writing program at Goddard, to channel his spirit guides. Beth, a fellow first semester student I have befriended, sits beside me cross-legged on the rug.

"You'll be fine," she tells me with the confidence of someone who has seen this sort of thing before. Even though I have just met Beth, I already feel a strong bond to this woman, and the four others we share meals with, like we are all soul sisters who have come together for this leg of our journey in life. l am already at home in this strange, yet beautiful, little college in rural Vermont.

When Peter's spirit guides enter the room, I feel the energy in the air rise, and my body quickens its shake. For the next thirty minutes my cells absorb the vibrations of the spirits as I listen to their translated words. They speak first of the shifting of the planet and of the collective pain that pervades Earth. Each word hits me with a wave of sadness, filling my body with a universal ache. My eyes spill with the tears of the planet and its people in crisis.

Next, Peter beings to go around the circle, asking each of us to stand and accept individual messages from spirit. When it is my turn, I find my feet and open my eyes. In this moment, I allow doubt to creep in and taunt me.

You are only hoping that this is for real, a dark shadow whispers inside my head.

Caught in the grasp of fear, I realize I have almost missed my message. The word "anger" catches me and pulls me back, and I quickly retrieve the words that came before it.

"You need to get rid of your anger," is the message I have received.

Peter is now pounding the right side of his belly, where I have long held a knot of ache. He is trying to find the source, saying the words stomach, spleen and liver before he moves onto the next person.

Now the tears that escape are all my own.

Guard seconds to battle

years. life

over-
shadowed by the past
fights to
travel back

to
love

One March day in 2009, I opened the mailbox to find a thin typed letter sandwiched between the household bills. It was addressed to Dave, from the National Guard. In a matter of seconds we learned our battle was finally over. The military had decided, finally, to grant Dave an honorable discharge. The eight years they wanted him to complete were up, and so was this long chapter in our life.

The letter was almost, after so long a wait, anticlimactic. The relief was over-shadowed by Dave's father's regular hospitalizations. Since the previous winter, after breaking his hip and suffering from pneumonia, my father-in-law's health had been in rapid decline. For six months Dave's father, and those visiting him, traveled back and forth from hospitals, to his home, and to rehab centers.

At the end of July, before I left for my second residency at Goddard, Dave, Ava, Alex, and I made our last trip to Massachusetts General Hospital where Dave's father was rapidly succumbing to congestive heart failure. The weather was warm and sunny, a perfect summer day. Ava, sensing the importance of the impending visit, was all business, while her brother complained about the long drive ahead and asked why we needed to go see Grandpa again.

My daughter chose a pink floral dress for the occasion, carefully matching it to a headband before she slipped her favorite sandals on her bare feet. Once she was satisfied with her appearance, Ava disappeared inside the privacy of the playroom, telling us she wanted to make a picture for her grandfather.

When she was finished, Ava and I went outside to cut a bouquet of flowers. While we walked through our gardens, my daughter and I debated the prettiest blooms not yet withered from the touch of sun. Ava, determined to give her grandfather roses, wanted to clip each flower she saw, but finally settled on two perfect pink blossoms after I reminded her of the smallness of the vase. To fill in the gaps between the roses, my daughter cut a handful of daises, and a sprig of coral bells, then tucked each stem tenderly into the mouth of the vessel, one at a time.

When it was time for us to leave for Boston, Ava stood by the door with the vase of flowers in one hand, and her over-sized picture in the other.

"What if we're too late?" she asked.

As I looked into my daughter's eyes I realized she knew, without having to be told, that this would be the last time she saw her beloved grandfather.

"We won't be," I replied as we shut the door to our home.

Every fifteen minutes or so, during the hour-and-a-half it took to reach her grandfather's room at Mass General, my daughter repeated her question. "What if we're too late?"

We paused at the glass doors of the room to wait for my mother-in-law, who stood beside her husband's bed, to beckon us in. Although I had watched his rapid decline over the last several months, I was struck by how pale and wasted my children's grandfather looked.

Overcome with an impulse to flee, I wanted to grab Ava and Alex's hands in mine, and head back down the hallway to the waiting elevator in an effort to shelter them from this last memory. Instead, I took their hands, and together, with their father, we walked inside. Alex, already over his limit of visits, edged past his grandfather's bed after a quick glance. For the next forty minutes he stayed planted by the window, asking repeatedly when we could leave, until mid-way through the visit he fell asleep in my arms.

When she entered the room, Ava released her hand from mine, and took the lead, pushing back her shoulders as she walked to the side of the bed. For ten minutes her eyes never wavered from her grandfather's face.

226

"Hi, grandpa," Ava said in a voice fortified with the strength of a granddaughter's love.

As my father-in-law slowly turned his head, I watched the pain in his face soften into recognition of his beloved granddaughter. Ava, in turn, proudly held up her vase of flowers and her over-sized sheet of drawing paper, so that he could see her gifts.

With her picture close to his face, Ava showed her grandfather the two figures drawn with blue marker. Pointing to the page, she explained how they were together in her drawing, holding hands. Granddaughter and grandfather stood beside a blue circle lake. In that moment, the two of them returned to their beloved cottage on a warm summer day to gaze across the water, while they listened for the haunting lyrics of loons.

After Ava was finished showing her gifts to her grandfather, she joined her brother and me on the chairs by the window. It was now my husband's turn. As I sat with my children looking out at the gray sky and the gray buildings, I listened to the strain in Dave's voice. Frustration mingled with love and heartache as my husband tried to talk with a father already half inside another world.

When my husband asked our children to visit with their grandfather again, Alex stuck fast to his chair, his eyes fixed on the red crane that hovered over a building behind the glass, refusing to budge. Instead, Ava hopped to attention and claimed the empty stool her father had just vacated, taking her grandpa's hand inside her two palms.

For several minutes my daughter sat beside her grandfather. As he drifted in and out of wakefulness, his hand would slip from her grasp. Each time it lost her hold, Ava would find it again. With her grandfather's hand in hers, Ava told him stories. His eyes closed to the rest of the world, my father-in-law absorbed his granddaughter's love through touch and words. Starting backwards, my daughter

227

took him through her morning picking flowers, to the day before swimming in the pool with her brother, and to two days prior playing with her cousins, until she ran out of recent memories. Then, with her eyes lifted to the window, Ava described the view he could not see. With words, she painted the sky and the tall buildings gray, the crane that hung its metal head over the city, red. Never once did my little girl, who was, on this day, only five-and-a-half-years-old, waver in her demonstration of love for her grandfather.

Three days later, before the break of dawn, the alarm clock in my bedroom went off at the same time my father-in-law's spirit left his body. The phone call from my husband at the hospital, minutes later, was almost unnecessary. In those early hours of morning, while Dave was preparing to leave the hospital and his father for the last time, I wept. I wept for my husband who had lost his father. I wept for my children who had to say their first goodbye to a beloved grandparent, and I wept for the little girl named Alethea who had tried so hard not to love her own grandfather too much.

The following day I left for Goddard with a heart filled with guilt. I would return home in three days for the funeral and wake, but had decided to go back to school again to finish up my week of residency. Although we had been anticipating his death for several months, I couldn't help but feel my father-in-law's passing was ill-timed, forcing me to choose between family and school. My husband and children, I knew, needed me, and I didn't want to leave them, but I also didn't want to stay. I couldn't let go of my dream. If I took off the whole week, I'd have to extend my studies for another semester. I was fortunate to have been granted this short leave.

The rest of the summer passed in the shadow of three deaths that occurred in my husband's family: his father's, the family dog, and an uncle. I felt the shadow of loss around me, and deeply within the cells of my body I felt my own shadows searching for light.

One day, late that summer while I was checking my email, I clicked open a request forwarded by a friend. There before me were two dogs, one the color of milk chocolate, the other a creamy white, sitting together with their faces peering into mine. I was sure they were saying "take me home." I clicked "reply" before I told my family.

That evening, when I presented the image of the two dogs in need of a home to my husband, he met my enthusiasm with caution.

"What makes you want a dog all of the sudden?" he asked skeptically. "Never mind two of them..." He knew me only as a cat lover.

"I'm not sure," I said, "but I do."

And I did. Suddenly it was all I could think about, this idea of getting a dog, or two. The child afraid of canines, and the woman who considered them a smelly nuisance, had vanished without warning.

The family who was seeking a new home for their two labs never emailed me back. I was more devastated than I let on. So were the kids. Until one day, at the beginning of August, my sister-in-law texted my husband a photo. A new arrival had appeared at the animal shelter where she volunteered. The dog, a malamute-collie mix named Veronica by the staff, peered through the camera with dark eyes covered in a face of fawn-colored fur. She reminded me of Nutmeg, only fluffier. I didn't need to see another dog. As I looked into those wise brown eyes, I knew she was waiting for me, just as I had been waiting for her.

The next day my kids and I hopped into our minivan, picked up my mother-in-law along the way (Dave was at work), and drove to the shelter. Ava and I met Veronica through the holes in her outdoor enclosure. To reach her, we had to pass a queue of dogs in cages, who protested our arrival by barking and lunging their bodies

229

against their chain-linked doors. Alex, petrified, turned around and headed back to the car with his grandmother, while I continued on with Ava and my sister-in-law, who had been waiting for us at the shelter. When we got to Veronica's cage, she was the only dog not barking. In fact, she barked only once during our visit, turning her head in the direction of the other dogs to issue one loud reprimand, as though commanding them to settle down while she got to know us.

"Be careful, Ava," I told my daughter as she fearlessly approached Veronica's cage. "Don't put your fingers through the holes."

My worry was unfounded. Veronica only wanted to be loved and touched. When she saw my daughter approach, she stuck her black nose through a hole for Ava to pet it. The bond between my daughter, who had wanted a dog since she could say the word, and Veronica, was sealed. There was no turning back. I too had fallen in love.

Dave and Alex, who had yet to meet Veronica, were easily persuaded that we needed to take her home. Her picture alone was iresistible. For the next week, we waited for the phone to ring. Impatient, we called the shelter every couple of days to get a status. Although my sister-in-law had ensured that we were first on the adoption list, there was a chance that Veronica's owners would show up and take her home. The law required us to let two weeks pass, so we did.

When the call finally came, we went shopping. We bought a pink collar and matching leash, along with a large dog bed, food, and bags of treats. I was in heaven shopping for the pet I couldn't wait to take home. Dave found a crate on Craig's List and we were good to go. Except, we needed a name. Veronica, we all agreed, didn't fit our new family member.

Ava immediately took charge, listing flowers off the top of her head.

"What about Daisy?" I suggested, recalling a woman who had once told my daughter, after she had picked her a bouquet of the blooms, that daisies are the happiest flower. We all agreed the name was perfect for our new pet.

A week before my birthday, my children and I returned to the shelter to take Daisy home. When my sister-in-law led her into the lobby, Daisy passed by several cats in cages without even a sideways glance, and headed straight for us.

"Now, she might be nervous about going into the van," my mother-in-law warned as we clipped the pink leash onto Daisy's collar and exited the shelter.

I clicked the button to slide open the minivan door, and Daisy took the lead, increasing her gait to a trot, and beating us all to her new vehicle. After hopping into the van, Daisy promptly claimed the back row of seats and looked at us. "Okay, let's get the show on the road," she seemed to be telepathically broadcasting.

"Guess I had nothing to worry about," my mother-in-law laughed as she helped buckle the kids into their seats.

By the time my husband came home from work, we had already given Daisy her first shampoo. As his car pulled up to the house, Daisy went to the door to wait, her tail wafting peppermint and the scent of wet dog through the kitchen. Aside from pooping on the front lawn, then rolling in it immediately after we got home, our new pet was already becoming comfortable into her new environment.

Daisy, though, had fooled us in two respects at the shelter. Her quiet demeanor switched to a barking defense each time someone or something she didn't know or trust approached her van, family or home. Soon we were calling her our "fierce protector."

We learned to tolerate the barking, viewing it as a mostly positive trait akin to an alarm system. What was harder to accept and remedy, though, was the prey drive that would turn on each time Daisy saw our cats. Penny and Yoda, who once enjoyed free-range of the house, quickly learned to steer clear of the new intruder in their home.

In an attempt to bring peace to the household, Dave installed cat doors in the basement and the garage, and I called a trainer. Penny and Yoda soon opted for living in the basement and outdoors, sneaking to the top floor only on chilly nights to cuddle on our bed. It soon became apparent that our six-year-old dog was not going to easily, if ever, out-grow her prey drive towards the cats.

"Malamute's a strong breed," the trainer told me when I grew frustrated. "She may never be able to coexist with the cats."

For a week we considered taking Daisy back to the shelter. Each member of our family was in turmoil, especially me. We loved Penny and Yoda, and felt guilty that we had violated their freedom by bringing a dog that didn't want to make friends with cats into our home. What had I done, I wondered? But my attachment to Daisy was visceral. The bond so quickly formed between us was deeply imbedded into my being, and the thought of giving up on Daisy and returning her to the shelter she had so desperately wanted to leave, was too much for me to bear. I couldn't repeat the mistakes of my childhood. I couldn't give up on another pet.

Besides, Daisy and I were already stubbornly in love. We needed each other. I, perhaps, needed her much more than she needed me. I could not imagine life without her. She was my constant companion, my teacher, and my best-friend.

"She's your dog, isn't she?" my husband's mother and sister would say to me with tones of awe when they saw us together, surprised and delighted by our strong bond.

My husband was even more amazed, "I cannot believe how much Daisy changed you. You went from someone who couldn't stand being around dogs to this. You love that dog more than you love me." He would often joke.

Not more, I thought, *but a little differently.* While Dave was teaching me the gift of unconditional love in the form of my beloved, Daisy embodied a love that spanned the barrier of species and language. With her constant, unwavering devotion, my new companion allowed me to realize that a bond can be formed so deeply between two beings, that there is no need for words.

I like to think I had been waiting for the day Daisy would enter my life, even though I was not consciously aware of it, and that she had been waiting for me to take her home. The time I missed not having a dog was quickly made up as I discovered the gifts that came from loving Daisy. The two of us spent our days together while Dave was at work and the kids were at school. With Daisy leading the way, we walked through forests to discover the beauty and wisdom held in nature. With my "fierce protector" beside me, my childhood fear of the woods and its shadows disappeared. In its place, I found a world filled with magic. A world, if I reached far enough back in time, I had once glimpsed with wonder through a child's eyes.

Daisy and I shared the quiet beauty of a peace where no words are needed. I learned to read her silent language, stopping to listen to the wisdom and magic of the natural world when Daisy stopped abruptly, refusing to budge until I went into the space of awareness. She gave me an unconditional love and devotion I had never before felt. Whenever we were parted, our eyes mirrored the joy of our reunion. I couldn't imagine my life without her.

At the end of August, I celebrated my 36th birthday with my family of four, plus three pets. While Daisy ran with my laughing children and husband on the lawn, I planted roses in my front yard. My mind traveled to memories of watching Grammie clipping back the decayed blooms of her beloved plants while a skinny brown cigarette dripped ashes like tears from her mouth. I smiled, recognizing our shared love for these beautiful flowers, as I formed a bridge with rocks to join my new garden with the irises and lilies. While I dug and planted, Yoda supervised me and Daisy, who was running around the yard on a leash pulled by my children. Surrounding me was everything I loved most, and on this birthday I did not weep.

Light

cut a halo through the black - panic

is perched on the edge
calm my body
hold me safe
I
want
to learn courage

addy, Daddy, Daaaady!" My four-and-a-half-year-old son's voice shattered our dreams. It was 2:00 a.m. and Alex had woken from another nightmare. My husband's unofficial role as first responder brought him to the side of our son's bed. Alex, full of sweat and delirium, was holding onto the image of fear he'd been battling in his sleep, calling out for his father to save him while he jumped up and down on his bed. With each cry, my heart skipped a beat.

"Alex, Alex! Settle down. What's wrong?" My husband's voice carried the exhaustion and frustration of routine as he attempted to calm our son.

I stayed in bed, my breath held tight in my stomach. On this night, the monster that pulled my son from slumber refused to leave him, and images of my own childhood night-terrors flashed through my mind. I saw forests filled with shadows. I saw an amorphous monster trying to capture two sisters who cowered in fear. This re-occurring dream of my childhood was relived as I wondered what terror my own child dreamt each night.

Down our short hallway, Alex continued to plead with my husband, who was holding fast to his insistence that our son needed to try to go back to sleep on his own. I followed their voices as they vied for control. Alex, fearing the dark of night with a desperate, undefinable fear I knew well, was begging his father, "Don't leave me Daddy. *Please Daddy, don't leave!*"

"Alex, lie down. You need to go back to sleep. You just had a bad dream," my husband countered with firmness. Tonight, I realized, he was not going to give in. His own fear that his son would not grow up to be strong and independent had won over his compassion.

Dave, who would have to rise again in a few hours with enough energy to tend to a day filled with other people's needs, was losing his patience.

"Alex, if you don't calm down and go back to sleep, I'll take your nightlight away."

The fear of losing his only source of light in the night — the small white flame that cut a halo through the blackness in his room — increased the panic in Alex's voice.

Fifteen feet away, I was now perched on the edge of my bed, sending silent pleas to my son to calm down while every neuron in my body fired the call to rescue. The need to hold my son in my arms in the safety of my bed was nearly overwhelming. Some nights, I resisted. This night, I held off as long as I could. There was also a part of me that wanted my son to learn courage at a young age and to discover how to survive, like I once had to, through a night of nightmares.

Alex, giving up on his father, called out to me in a desperate attempt to be saved. I could not bear my child's terror for one more moment. I could not let him endure a night without light, so I jumped out of bed.

"Go back to sleep," I told my husband firmly, scooping our son into my arms.

"You're not helping him," Dave grumbled his defeat as he made his way back to our room.

I could feel Alex's breath slow down against my chest, along with his heart-rate. His tears stopped moistening my shoulder, as he clutched tight to my neck.

While I walked the perimeter of the bedroom, holding my son, I became aware of how heavy he had become. No longer could I hold my youngest child easily on one hip. Instead, I had to support his weight against my chest, lacing my hands under his bottom. His long arms circled awkwardly my neck. His legs hung loose, like anchors, toward the floor as he began to relax into a state near sleep.

I peered into every shadow cast by the tiny, exposed bulb of Alex's nightlight (we took the cover off weeks before, submitting to his request for more light). The room was almost too bright, the bare bulb bringing definition to each object in the room. I wondered if this was part of the problem. I could not sleep in a room that bright. Alex, though, would have it no other way.

While I walked him around his room, I asked my child about his fears, but in response he told me only that he was scared. I shifted his weight in my arms, bringing his body closer. Silently, I prayed to a universal God I was beginning to believe in, asking for courage. Asking that my son find strength to ward off the darkness that he feared so deeply.

My daughter, like her mother once did, made a habit of using her stuffed animals as guards. Each night she would arrange the biggest and bravest along the sides of her body, tucking at least two on either side of her head. She used pillows to fill in gaps, and then drew her quilt over her head. On my way to my own bed each night, I had a routine that involved folding down the quilt, and kissing the top of Ava's warm head, while I waited for her next breath to release.

My son also used blankets for protection, wrapping them around his head. It was a fierce wrap though, with just his face exposed and turned toward the bulb plugged into the wall. He stared into the illuminated night. My daughter shut it out.

We paced the room for several more minutes, and while I held my son in my tired arms his sleepy voice tried to convince me to crawl with him into his bed. There were nights when I did. I wanted to that night, just as I did all the others, but instead I reminded Alex, again, that there were no monsters in our house. That Daisy, our "fierce protector," would scare them away before they could get past the door. I told my son that if Daisy barked at the chipmunks on the lawn, and the crows in the trees, she would surely bark at anyone, or thing that didn't belong in the house. I reminded him that his sister was just next door, and his father and I, a few steps down the hall. We were all here to protect him, and each other, I told him as I pleaded with Alex to try to sleep, and finally he did.

After months of broken sleep, Alex overcame his night terrors. While he was outgrowing these fears, mine were lingering. As I watched my children adjust to life, my childhood insecurities returned to me.

One day, my stepfather decided to hang two bucket swings from the beam of his breezeway so his grandchildren could swing out, over the brick into the open air. I calculated the probability of a fall. I looked up at the wooden beam, and noted the cracks that had formed from the turns of the screws, following the thick, white ropes down to where they tied into knots, two holding each swing. Nervously, I asked my stepfather if he was sure the anchored ropes would hold my children's weight.

"Of course they will, Alethea. I would never let them fall," he said with a firm voice that bordered on reprimand. *But,* I thought, *you once let me fall.*

Inside my mind I saw a nine-year-old child falling from her homemade bunkbed that lacked a safety railing, onto the hard surface of the wood floor four-and-a-half feet below. I sucked in my lower lip and felt the lingering line of the white scar, reminding me where my teeth had punctured through the soft tissue of my face. I felt the click of the jaw that had nearly broken, as I opened a mouth that was still afraid to question my stepfather.

For more than four years, I watched my children swing, my son in a blue chair, my daughter in a plastic blue fish, over the brick threshold and out past the rocks that led onto my parents' lawn. With each push from my stepfather's thick arms, my breath would build inside a constricted chest until it burst for release. The ropes never gave out, but held fast, as promised, to the beam. My children, in their swings, would laugh in the wind, screaming past my worried face, "Higher, Gampy! Higher!"

Ava and Alex's courage grew with time, and they began to release their hands from the ropes, as the impact of their grandfather's push sent their bodies swaying to the sides in a curved trajectory.

One day, when my son was four, he slipped halfway out of the seat after a push from his grandfather. The seat was now much too small for his long body. A rush of hands (including mine) reached out to prevent Alex's fall onto the bricks. In that terrifying moment, I calculated the force of the impact of his body, pulled by gravity, against the hard lip of the bricks below.

My nerves had finally reached their limit. The timid comments I had been making with increased frequency about the safety of my children inside the swings were being dismissed as frivolous worry. I felt as though I was the only one who could see the danger lurking, now made glaringly apparent by Alex's near fall. My voice, though, was not strong enough to be heeded.

Instead, another near accident, unrelated to the swings, finally resulted in their removal from the hooks in the beams.

We were driving in the car when Ava, who had recently turned six, told me about crossing the ice-covered stream near her grandparents' house. As she walked over it, she told me, the ice beneath her cracked and opened, pulling her body into the rushing water.

"That sounds scary," I told her as my heart skipped a beat, "but you don't have to worry. It was just a dream."

"I think I know why I had the dream," my daughter offered. My grip on the steering wheel tightened as I listened to Ava narrate her most recent visit with her grandparents. Against the backdrop of the black road ahead of me, I saw my daughter playing in the snow with her four-and-half-year-old brother and a seven-year-old boy from across the road. I watched them sledding down the snowy hillside together onto the ice of my parents' pond.

"Did you have your helmets on?" I asked her.

"No, Gammy never put them on."

"Where was Gammy when you were sledding?" I asked.

"She was outside with us and then she got too cold and went inside."

My daughter continued her story, explaining that after a while she had grown tired of sledding and asked the two boys to go over to the stream on the other side of the house. In my mind, I pictured her leading the way up the embankment of the pond, over the plowed driveway, to cross behind the garage to get to the stream.

"After Christopher and I helped Alex across, the ice cracked, and I got scared," she told me.

I gripped the steering wheel in an attempt to balance the emotion in my voice. "You know, honey," I told my daughter. "You shouldn't cross the stream even when it has ice on it. The ice could break. It's dangerous. You should have used the bridge."

"So you all crossed over?" I urged her to continue. "What happened next?"

"Yes, but after the ice cracked I got scared, so we went back over the bridge, and I went inside and told Gammy what happened."

"Ava," I said again, "you know you really shouldn't have crossed the stream. And," I added, "Gammy shouldn't have gone inside without you."

"It wasn't Gammy's fault," Ava quickly interjected. "It was my idea to cross the stream."

"But you're only six, Ava. What if the ice had cracked all the way through, like in your dream?"

After my children were in bed that night I told my husband Ava's story, and together we composed an email to my parents. "By the way," I added at the end, "my children are no longer allowed to swing on the breezeway." I had finally found the conviction I needed to communicate these words, even though I had opted to write them.

The swings were gone the next time we went to my parents' home, but the incident beside the stream had escalated into a battle for truth that would never be fully resolved.

"Yes, I went inside," my mother eventually confessed. "I was cold, but I was watching them from the window the entire time."

"I didn't put their helmets on," she admitted, "because I can't seem to remember to do that when they're sledding, only when they're riding bikes." A jab I felt, as I knew my mother and stepfather thought both my sister and I were over-protective of our children.

"But they're ski helmets. I brought them over specifically for sledding," I reminded her.

My mother never explained the gap in time, the five minutes it must have taken for all three children to walk up the driveway, cross behind the garage, and walk over the stream.

"I came out when I saw Ava crossing the stream and yelled at them to come inside," she told me instead.

"Where was dad?" I finally asked.

"In his office working. I was in charge of the kids."

I thought about my stepfather's office, and how its windows overlooked the stream and the yard beside the garage. It seemed unlikely, to me, that he would not have heard and seen the children outside, crossing over the stream. My mother, though, was still his most loyal defender, and I, his fearful daughter.

I also thought about a summer day when my daughter was only eighteen months old. She had been walking with my stepfather beside the pond, looking for frogs, when she slipped on the steep bank and fell face first into the water. I saw her tiny body once again, prone and spread-eagle, sinking against the murky surface. I recalled my mother's words spoken on that day, "It figures Ava would be the first to fall in." I remember how my stepfather, after my sister and I had yelled at him from across the pond, had reached into the water to rescue my daughter before he stormed inside the house without a word.

My mother, I realized, would once again not let her husband take any blame. She was too accustomed to protecting him, and she was, I knew, like me, afraid of his wrath. *If she never protected me, how can I trust her to protect my children?* I finally began to ask myself.

"Can you tell me again what you remember from that day?" I asked Ava again.

Her story stayed the same.

"It's my fault, though," she added.

I asked her brother if this was what he remembered, and he told me it was.

Choosing my words in an effort not to tarnish their image of their grandparents, I said, "Gammy told me she came outside when she saw you crossing the stream, and that Alex and Christopher never crossed it. Did you all go over the stream, and did Gammy come outside, or did you go inside to get her?"

"We all went over the stream, and I went inside after I heard the ice crack," Ava told me. Alex again confirmed his sister's words.

"But," Ava added, "it wasn't Gammy's fault. It was my idea to cross the stream."

Days later, I dreamt of a dark forest.

Trees bend and tangle bare arms into an arch. The doorway is a light of gold over a tunnel of darkness I know I must enter. There is something for me inside I need to find.

I step through the parting of the trees and begin to run along a dark path. My white nightshirt flaps above my naked waist. I don't feel the hard bumps of the ground when they meet the soft skin of my feet. I am too focused on the light, and the knowing that at some point, the shadows of the forest will end, and the trees will open to it.

The forest releases me into a white room that grows before my eyes. It is filled with strangers. The space expands into a building; a warehouse of rooms and more people. I don't know where to go, and suddenly I am aware of my half-naked body and the wild in my hair and face. They must see it too, these strangers, but they don't seem to care that I am here. It is as though they do not see me. These people, who all look alike, and talk with each other as though only they belong. Everyone, it seems, knows why they are here, except me.

I stop a man. The hair on his head is short and black, the color of the mustache above his mouth. He is not tall. His face, when turned toward me, does not smile, but it is not unkind. "Where is the path?" I ask. "Will you lead me to it?" The man looks into my face showing me his concern with eyes that try to read my need.

"Are you sure you want to go there?"

"Yes," I tell him. "Yes. I need to go back."

He takes me outside, through a door I have not noticed at the end of the building. The beginning of the path is not far. The forest is waiting for me. This time, when I enter, I am not alone. I have found a child who looks like my daughter. I lift her weight, and she rides upon my back, her small arms laced around my neck.

Now I am running to beat time. I know I must carry my child through the forest before the darkness closes in upon us, shutting out all light. I feel the presence of evil waiting in the shadows for me to lose the path, waiting to grab my daughter away from me. Tangled snares of roots try to stumble my feet into their hold. I will not let my daughter slip. My arms cannot lose her weight as I run faster and faster through the darkness.

Up ahead I see a pure white form shaped into the body of a unicorn. The size of a pony with the density of a cloud, the unicorn floats through darkness crossing our path. It stops at the edge of the shadows, turning, ready to leap toward us. This brilliant being of beauty startles me. I am, I realize, afraid of the energy that could be transferred by the brush of its white body against my skin. My heart speeds its wild beat inside my chest. Beyond the unicorn I can see the trees where they arch around the golden body of the sun. We are almost there. We are almost safe.

I woke from the dream before I made it through the doorway of light, with my heart pounding the rhythm of my dream feet. While I tried to slow my breath in the darkness of my room, my mind lingered on my daughter. Even though my dream was over, I could not escape the impulse to save and protect.

I thought about stealing into Ava's bedroom to pull her out of the warmth of her covers, and bring her into my bed. I had done this once or twice when she was a baby, too young to remember, surrounding my body with her warmth after my dreams had threatened to take her from me.

She probably wouldn't mind, I reasoned. My daughter whose love was as fierce as my own, I knew, would understand. Instead I let her sleep, telling myself that she was safe. Later, as the sun began to cover the darkness of night with its golden skin, I wondered about the child in the forest. That little girl riding upon my back who looked, I realized, too much like me.

Later that day I walked the town's woods with Daisy by my side, as I had grown accustomed to doing. The body of my beloved companion, when I looked down at her, glowed with a purple aura. My senses, I realized, were keenly alert, my heart felt wide open. Nature responded in kind. I could feel the breath of the wind as my own. The birdsong stirred the harmony of my heart into a place that felt like a long-forgotten home. Under a cathedral of pines and oaks, I released the dam holding my fears. As I wept, the energy of the elemental kingdom washed me clean in currents of love. I felt peace. Beneath one's feet, I discovered, the Earth's heart beats to heal. Its rhythm is love.

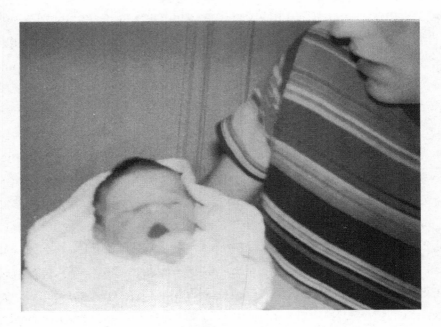

Father

imagine
sadness
anger rising like a
futile wave

find
me

in words and in the space between them

I wrote my first letter to my father when I was thirty-six. As a child I remember sending the perfunctory Christmas and birthday cards to him, but those cards quickly dwindled after our annual visits stopped. They were always sent with a mix of guilt, anger, and resentment. Now, fifteen years after I had last seen my father, I was ready to make a connection. I was working on this story of my truth, missing gaps of information that could only come from him. It was the excuse I needed to learn more about a man I had been taught to believe never loved me.

Perhaps if he had an email address, I would have sent an email, but I like the tangibility of words on paper. Content, typed in black ink against the white expanse of a letter, has formality in its shape and lends to the value of the message being sent and the hope of a reply. It was not an easy letter to write. I was not sure how to begin to cross the wide river of silence we had created so long ago. What words would I choose to link together a bridge of reunion?

I began formally with *Dear*, followed by the word that never felt right, *Dave*. I told him about going to graduate school for creative writing. *For the first time in my life I know beyond any doubt I am where I am supposed to be,* I wrote. In that small, progressive college in rural Vermont, I had found a home.

Next, I told my father I was writing a memoir, knowing these words could only bring him to places he might prefer to forget. I wanted him to remember me as a young child. I wanted him to realize the life he had missed. *It has not been an easy journey,* I wrote, *the pains of the past are still sharp, but it is a necessary journey that is allowing me to heal.* With these words I gave my father an invitation to help me lay down the trusses.

I also needed my father to feel the pain of our shared loss, as well as the possibility of redemption, so I told him, As you know, we have not had an easy relationship, and I write this letter not knowing how you will respond. Beyond the occasional phone conversation, we do not really know each other. Perhaps this can be an opportunity for discovery for both of us.

Before I closed the letter, I asked for my father's memories, hoping that he would offer the past through the open shade of his truth. I signed my name under Love, and then sent my words three thousand miles away to a small coastal town in Washington.

After he moved there, my father sent me a photograph of his home in Ocean Park. It was strange for me to imagine him living in a house that was not his mother's. Along with the photograph, he sent a picture of his partner, Pam. She was the first girlfriend I had known him to have since my mother left him. I had never met her. There was so much that I didn't know about the father of my birth.

My father's house, in the picture, looked old and quaint, a one-and-a-half-story white bungalow shuttered against the winds of the coast. I could see why he liked living here, with its antique charm (he was, after all, his mother's son), and proximity to the wild beauty of the ocean. When my father started calling me more often, after the births of my two children, he would sometimes tell me about digging for clams with Pam's grown kids and young grandchildren when the tide was low, and I wondered if he was speaking in code about our loss.

When I looked at the image of Pam, I compared her to my mother. Like Pam, my mother once had curly brown hair, but hers was lighter before it turned gray, the curls looser before she cut them short. I searched Pam's face for the beauty of my mother, but saw only the large brown eyes of a stranger.

I was surprised by how soon my father responded to my letter with a phone call. I heard the distinct notes of hope and pleasure in his voice as he told me how happy he was to have received my letter. From here, he turned quickly back to his own childhood, sharing with me memories of picking beans at nearby farms for spending money as a young boy, and playing baseball with his friends after school. While he talked, I wondered if we would make it to the year when I entered his life. I was looking for facts, but I was also looking for a sign of love to bring me into his world.

When my father reached the moment when he met my mother, my attention sharpened. I listened closely to his memory of the dance they attended at a church that neither of them belonged to. His words offered little that I didn't already know, and it was not easy for me to visualize an attraction that brought my parents together. My father moved onto his memories of attending college at Portland State, where he majored in English, while still dating my mother "off and on," until in his junior year when she became pregnant with my sister.

As I listened to my father recall his story, I compared his words to those of my mother, and my mother's mother, who have both shared versions of this past when my young parents struggled with the responsibility of unplanned marriage and children. My father's words, filled with self-sacrifice, followed more closely the words of my grandmother who has always sympathized with him.

I thought about the stories my mother would tell me of the time after she became pregnant with my sister. Her voice, laced with contempt for a man who was more concerned about making sure his own closet was filled with clothes and shoes, than caring properly for his young family, echoed in the recesses of my mind. Each individual's story, I realized, holds a truth in some form. A truth that helped to shape who I was.

I pressed the receiver to my ear. My father's disjointed memories were hard to follow along the bumpy path of his nervous voice. I listened while he skipped over my birth to the year when I was two, and my mother left him without warning to disappear into a life

251

with the Hare Krishnas. Again, while he spoke, my mother's words came back to me. In my mind, I could see my father creeping through the windows of a house where he was no longer welcome, like a burglar, rummaging through drawers and closets while we were away.

Was it during one of these uninvited visits, I wondered, that he discovered we were not coming back? My mother had always left out the part when he tried to find us, and as my father spoke, I brought pencil to paper and tried to make note of the nervous jumble and mumble of his thoughts.

I listened to my father's voice struggle with memory as it traveled more than three decades back in time. The distance he tried to cover in his speech was a nonlinear search, interjected with comments such as "That was a crazy time," along with asides about the papers and letters he had kept and stored away in boxes in his attic.

While my father spoke, I focused my thoughts on an image of him driving his brown Ford truck through Washington and into Canada with his sister Linda, still a teenager, in the seat beside him. I tried to imagine a look of frustration on his face; brows furrowed with sadness and disappointment, as he realized the futility of the false lead he had received. I imagined his anger too, rising like a futile wave when he learned from my grandmother that we were actually somewhere in California.

When my father arrived at the point of giving up, I felt the momentary impulse to ask why the long search, only to let us go. Later, I received an answer when he offered these words in reference to the time when our court-ordered visitations had ceased, "I know it probably seemed like I abandoned you," he said, "but I knew you had a good life in New Hampshire. "Besides," he added, "I had my family at the zoo." My father never said anything about me abandoning him.

I tried to digest my words as they mixed uncomfortably with my own truth, and realized there was no way for me to reply without showing him a long childhood filled with loss and guilt. Now, mixed with this, was a realization that only a parent who had been estranged, at least partially at will from his children, could hold onto this type of compromised belief. *I had my family at the zoo.* The words now imprinted inside of my brain felt cold and distant.

My father started talking again about the attic where, stored among the papers and letters, were photographic negatives he promised to find and send to me. I thought about the album displayed outside in the sun on a table at my aunt Linda's in the summer of 1995. The last day my father and I had seen each other.

Once again, while my father spoke, I tried to find myself in his words, and in the space between them. In my mind, I shaped the image of his second baby girl, the one born at a house that looked like a gray-and-white milk carton, the single-serving kind. When we finally spoke of this day, my father told me it was sunny. For the first time, I interjected, mentioning that perhaps he might be wrong, because my mother remembers the clouds, and the grayness of Oregon rain in summer. Still, my father insisted upon the sun, and his memory that it was shining on the day of my birth. For confirmation, he mentioned the possibility of calling my maternal grandmother to find out if he was right. The sun, though, didn't really matter to me. I had already committed my mind to the rain. I could see the gray mood it created for the scene of my birth. How it darkened the small room, and cast shadows upon the bed where I was released from my mother's body into an uncertain world.

While my father negotiated with the weather, I pictured a baby girl coming into an uncertain life. I saw the shadow of her eight-and-a-half-pound-body, and watched as she was brought near the window, where her gray, slippery skin was wiped of her mother with a clean, white towel until she shined pink and new. I watched and waited for the moment when the contours of her face would be revealed.

I thought about asking my father why he had never chosen a new middle name, a girl's name, after I was born. I thought of telling him about the story of the young woman whose face bloomed into the deep shade of shame each time "Eamon" was shouted with laughter, ricocheting off hallways like needles, when she was in the eighth grade. A part of me wanted to show him how much weight a name carries. Perhaps, though, he already knows this. A father whose own daughters, when they were too young to remember, stopped calling him dad.

The second time my father phoned me after I sent him the letter, I was writing a narrative about the day of the picnic when he asked me and my sister what we wanted to call him. It was one of those uncanny moments when our thoughts seem to beckon the person inhabiting our minds. This time, my father called to inquire if I had a chance to look at, and possibly develop, some of the photographic negatives he had sent to me. Although I had in my possession this batch of about two hundred miniature images on film for three weeks, I still hadn't figured out what to do with them. At the time of my father's call, I was overwhelmed by the sepia ghosts from our past, which appeared each time I held the strips of film to light. My reply was not what he had hoped for.

"I am not sure what to do with them yet," I told him. "It's hard for me to sort through and figure out what is in the images."

What I really wanted to do was ask my father for the developed photographs, but I felt it would be too great a request. That if he wasn't ready to part with them fifteen years ago at my Aunt Linda's, he wouldn't want to now. I also understood that my father, by sending me the negatives, was trying to help me piece together my past in the best way he knew how to. After I told him I had not developed any of the pictures yet, and was still trying to decipher their unlabeled contents, he offered more memories over the phone.

"Did you see the ones of the A-frame we lived in in Cave Junction?" he asked.

I told him no, the undeveloped images must have been too dark.

"I thought I saw a tepee in one. Was it ours?" I asked, because my mother had never told me we had lived in a tepee before Henniker. I was anxious to hear if my father would offer some new information.

"No, that was your mom's friend, Maya's," he replied.

While I mulled this information over in my mind, trying to recall what I already knew about Maya, a woman I remember who wore saris and once gave me and my sister our own, my father released a nervous laugh. "Did you see the one of your sister standing in a closet holding a pot?"

"No, I don't think so," I replied a little annoyed, wondering why a photo of my sister holding a flower pot in front of a closet would have been noteworthy, until I realized I had not heard him correctly. That instead of just "a pot," he must have said, "a pot plant," because he then began talking about growing marijuana in flower pots in the back yard, and hiding them amid the tomato plants. I couldn't share his amusement. Instead, I thought of the tie that bound my two fathers together, and the plants they had both tried to hide, pretending they were tomatoes. I was not, I realized, angry with him, though. There was a strange comfort to my father's openness, and his candid sharing of a truth I had known about, in fragmented form, since I was a young child. It was not a secret he was trying to hide from me, or deny.

The trip west

time
ask me
for memories

resuscitate
truth
walk to meet me

S even months after I sent my father the letter, I boarded a plane destined for Oregon with my husband and two children. The entire trip west, including the stop-over in Chicago, took twelve hours. Ava and Alex, caught up in the euphoria of this new adventure, never once complained. Instead, my daughter spent most of the flight listening to her mp3 player, looking out the window, and hopping over the seats to sit on my lap to read Nancy Drew, while father and son watched Transformers and played video games on a laptop computer. Despite my husband's bouts of motion sickness during the two take-offs and landings, it was a remarkably smooth set of flights.

Alex fell asleep for the final forty-five minutes of our journey, while Ava kept her eyes wide open until 1:30 a.m. eastern time, when we finally settled into our beds at the Ramada Inn near the airport.

This time, when I landed in Portland, my extended family was not there to greet me. My father, during our phone conversations before the trip, had hinted at the possibility of meeting us at the airport, by asking me the details of our flight. I was not ready for the memories that might surface by his welcoming presence, so I told him only that we would be arriving late. Very late. It was, after all, the truth.

When I fell asleep in the wee hours of the morning beside my son, dreams took the form of Margot and a mysterious lover. The lover came first, appearing as a stranger who bent down to kiss me full upon the lips three times. A number symbolic of creation, freedom, and harmony. The number for birth, and rebirth. With each touch of the lover's lips energy surged in currents of heat through my body, as though I were being resuscitated from a long lapse without breath. He left, as he had arrived, without warning. Then Margot appeared in the distance, walking as though to meet me. I could see the smile of friendship upon her lips. The same was on my own. When the distance between us grew small, I told her the vise that once gripped my chest had opened, and then, like the lover, she disappeared.

Guilt arrived before I was fully awake, threatening to swallow the energy the night had given me. My dreams now replaced by thoughts of my parents in New Hampshire, and remorse that I had dreamt of a lover who was not my husband, until I realized the lover was an archetype of love in human form, welcoming me back home. The restless body of my waking son pushed aside the remaining remnants of guilt, and I felt pure love reaching for my hands. My son, who like my daughter has the ability to read my emotions, took my hands to his lips and gave me three kisses. In that time between sleep and waking, when our minds connect more easily with the wisdom of our souls, my five-year-old son pulled his stuffed iguana, Max, from beneath his pillow and placed it upon my chest. Instinctively, I let my hand glide down its back. "Don't bend his scales," my son whispered beside me, "he needs his armor." And a part of mine, I thought, had just released.

We began our first day in Oregon visiting my maternal grandmother at her condo in Portland. The last time I had seen her, Poppy was still alive. My grandmother was waiting at the curb beside her building when we arrived, so close to the street I worried for a moment she might fall forward before we stopped the car. I noticed she had left the walker my mother had sent her as a gift inside the building.

My grandmother's feet moved fast, carrying her bent torso ahead of us in her rush to bring us into her home. When she unlocked the door to her condo, I noticed first the white of the rug that covered her floors, and told my children to remove their shoes, as I slipped off mine.

"Oh, don't worry about doing that," my grandmother said. "The rug needs to be cleaned anyway." I saw no spots.

My grandmother's home, now big enough for one, was devoid of dirt and dust. Order still reigned. While we sat together in her living room, my grandmother studied each of us. Ava, who had warmly greeted this great-grandmother she had never met, with a full embrace after she jumped out of the car, was moving from chair to chair, running her hands across the same cushions I had sat upon as a child. Each object that rested on a table or shelf within her reach, felt the touch of my daughter's fingers.

"Ava, settle down! Please be careful," I told her, fearing she would break the large cluster of amethysts Poppy had unearthed during one of his mineral digs.

"Don't worry," my grandmother laughed. "She's fine. I like watching her."

Alex, who refused to hug his great-grandmother and had asked to leave before we sat down, was now rolling a wooden train Poppy had carved across the carpet. As I watched him, I thought about how much my son was like the great-grandfather he would never meet. Not only did they share the same birthday, they also shared a love of creating with their hands in the quietness of their own space.

Later, my grandmother would tell me the wood my son was gliding across the floor was some of the last my grandfather's hands had touched. It would take her two months after we left to put the train back in its place under the coffee table. Preferring, instead, to gaze at in and think of us.

My grandmother, as she sat on the couch, followed my children with her eyes. "I feel like I'm in a dream," she whispered every few minutes. "I can hardly believe you are all here."

We got up to leave an hour later, eager to be on our way to the zoo, and the busy day ahead. After going to the zoo we had plans to meet up with my father, who would lead us to Pam's son's home for a family barbecue.

"We'll be back sometime tomorrow afternoon, after we go to the gorge, to pick you up," I told my grandmother, who showed me the paper bags she had already packed full of dried pasta, cereal, and pretzels for our six-night-stay together at the coast.

"What else would you like me to bring?" she asked me as she opened the doors to her cabinets and refrigerator. She still, I saw, kept enough food to feed a small army.

"What you've packed is enough, Gramma, we'll go shopping when we get there," I told her while Ava started pulling cans of peaches off her shelves.

"Do you want those? What else do you want?" My grandmother turned her attention to Ava. Pretzels, a jar of pink fruit juice, and boxes of macaroni made their way into shopping bags, along with the canned peaches before I managed to steer my enthusiastic daughter to the door.

The drive to the zoo was a mural of memories, but the original mural was old. It had been twenty-four years since it had been painted inside my mind, and time had altered it. Pieces had faded and fresh scenes had been added. While my husband battled the traffic, which I was certain had increased exponentially in my absence, I pieced together the landscape. There, a few miles before the exit, was the tunnel through the hillside covered with houses. Instinctively, I held my breath before we entered its dimly lit corridor.

Beside the highway, patches of ivy still invaded the hillsides, their green masses having spread over time. I recalled my father once telling me about a nickname he had been given, "the ivy man," for the futile war he tried to wage against this invasive plant. Ahead was the sharp curve of the exit wrapped with Oregon roses. Although we were early, the parking lot was already packed with cars, and two long lines of eager patrons filled the walkway leading to the gated entrance.

For five hours, I walked the paths of the zoo beside the animal-filled cages with my family, in a haze of memory. I watched the faces of my delighted children and thought about my childhood. Our last turn before the exit led us through the animals of Africa. There was a small crowd mingling among the viewing area outside an enclosure.

I found a gap and moved to the center of the gated handrails. Standing before me was a giraffe, her spotted pelt frozen against a backdrop of green leaves. Only her mouth moved in the lazy rock of chewing. The giraffe's elongated front legs crossed at the ankles in a picture of elegance. She watched me in silent witness as I captured her image twice with the click of my camera.

The gift shop had moved and grown in size since I last mingled through its aisles as a child. Ava, never able to resist the soft bodies of stuffed animals, spent her time trying to choose the cutest face among them, while my son found the hard orange head of a tiger, snapping its fierce teeth with the trigger mechanism beneath its poled body. "You can each choose one thing," I told them, echoing the words of my father so long ago.

In the parking lot, I took my cell phone out of my pocket, and found the number I had programmed in a few days before. My heart sped with its first ring, and I heard fifteen years of accumulated hope in my father's "hello."

During the drive to Troutdale, I strived for a casual tone as I turned my voice to the back- seat. "What would you like to call Mommy's birth-father?" I asked my children. My daughter immediately began weighing the options while my son snapped the teeth of his tiger. "I don't know," he said.

"Should we call him Grandpa?" Ava asked.

"Sure, if you want to. Or maybe you could call him Grandpa Dave," I suggested, thinking about my husband's father whom they had once called "Grandpa." It didn't seem right for them to share the same name, and I wasn't sure if I was ready for him to have the full title of grandfather. Alex replied by snapping the jaws of the plastic tiger head.

"If you want to," I said again as we pulled into the parking lot in front the Levi's outlet in Troutdale.

I held my breath each time I turned around to scan the entryway to the mall for arriving vehicles. Even though we had the windows lowered, I felt hot and confined. My heart raced. I looked at my children, ages five and six, sitting more calmly than their anxious mother in their back seats. Were they nervous? Excited? I couldn't fully read their faces. Alex appeared absorbed with his new toy. Ava was glowing, as she always does when something new is about to happen. She would be fine I decided.

I spotted his truck before it turned into the lot, and before I could read the logo on its side, or notice the crack that ran the length of the windshield in a pattern that made me think of lightning. The truck was old and white with a cab on its bed. As it turned, I read the word "Earthwhile," over a globe crossed with a shovel and rake. I thought of ivy spreading over the sides of the freeway. I thought of Grammie's roses. I thought of a childhood of losses that could never be fully recovered.

I smiled and waved my father over, watching as he stepped with a slight hesitation, but a face full of joy, out of his truck and towards the daughter he had not seen in fifteen years. Thirty-four years of fear and doubt disappeared as I embraced my father. He had never left me, I realized in that moment, but had only been waiting, quietly, for me to return home.

When I turned to open the back doors in an effort to release my children, Ava and Alex chose to stay inside. My daughter offered a shy smile, and a "hi," in response to my father's greeting. My son, an "I'm going to get you" with a snap of his tiger's mouth.

At the barbecue, Alex continued to hold fast to the handle of his new toy, snapping periodic threats through the air, until Lily, my father and Pam's black pug/chihuahua puppy, stole his attention away. Soon, my husband and I were timing turns with this irresistible distraction that both of our children could not get enough of.

As I looked around at the people gathered, I saw that it was in many ways easiest for the four of us who had traveled the farthest to be there. Pam, who played the part of eager hostess, read too deeply into my compliment about her son's smoked salmon and quickly produced more to replace the diminishing flakes. My father, who manned the barbecues, mumbled repeated reprimands at himself for the burnt hotdogs the children had passed over in favor of links fresh from the package. The chicken, in contrast, took too long to cook.

When he was not tending to the meat on the grill, my father chatted with my husband, each with a beer in hand, while I captured their images with a click of my camera. From my seat on the lawn, I watched Pam's grandchildren play with my children and marveled at how smoothly our families had come together in just a couple of hours.

My father's nervousness was slow to abate. Before we ate, he fumbled in the kitchen drawers for a wine opener. Then opting for a knife, he broke through the cork in the bottle, spraying burgundy like blood across the white of the tiled floor and the plastic window shade above the sink. Pam's daughter and I sprang into action, unraveling a roll of paper towels to absorb the red spots, until finally the shade was removed and rinsed with a hose.

Later, with my father beside me, I chewed squares of Tillamook cheddar and crackers, swallowing with memory, as we tried to condense time. I looked into my father's face, and he, in turn, studied mine. The eyes I thought were green, I saw, were really a mix of green and blue, like the anemones that cling to the rocks of the Oregon coast. The lines across his forehead had deepened through the years, and his once shaggy brown hair was now all gray and shorn close to his face.

"Is your sister's hair still lighter?" he asked me.

"No, it's been brown, like mine, for some time," I replied, with a spark of irritation as I wondered why he could not remember that it had only been light when she was a small child.

After we had eaten our plates of chicken, my father and I stood together again on the lawn, while we watched my husband chase the four children across the grass. I felt my father's arm wrap loosely around the back of my waist, as he turned to me and said, "You know, you really have something special."

"I know," I replied, feeling the full weight of his words.

The next day was July 17th, the eleven year anniversary of my marriage to Dave. Early in the day, we met up with my husband's younger brother who had been living in Portland for the last three years, and together the five of us drove along I-84 to Multnomah Falls. The weather was chilly, and the wind blew a constant gust across our bodies as we hiked through the crowds to see the waterfall.

Later, we collected my grandmother, her bags, and her walker, and headed west toward Lincoln City. The drive to the coast took much longer than we had anticipated. My grandmother directed my husband, who was driving, adding detours as she struggled to remember the way. She also, it became clear, wanted us to make an unplanned stop at her eldest son's home in Keizer, but we were fast approaching the dinner hour, and my family and I were becoming irritated from our hunger. We had not planned to visit with my aunt and uncle, and the idea of stopping in, unannounced, did not appeal to any of us, aside from my grandmother. We just wanted to find somewhere to eat.

My grandmother pointed us in the direction of her favorite casino, where, ravenous and slightly bewildered, we stood in an immense, cafeteria-style room piling Dungeness crab legs, egg rolls, pasta and sushi onto our plates. Ava was in her element, filling her stomach with sushi, crab dipped in drawn butter, and egg rolls before returning to the buffet to ruminate on the countless selections of pies, cakes and ice cream.

It was nearly 8:00 p.m. when we arrived at the rental house on Road's End. Before we unloaded all of our bags, the kids began asking if we could go down to the ocean. So, together the five of us walked to the beach as the sun melted into the water. While Ava and Alex raced with the wind near the water's edge, I traced their footprints until my eyes found the word "FREE" scratched into the sand in bold letters. A message that seemed fated filled my heart with the song of the ocean, and I turned into the wind to breathe in its salted breath.

Later, as we prepared for sleep in the privacy of our bedroom, my husband remarked with unmistakable disappointment, "That wasn't exactly the anniversary dinner I had hoped to have with you."

"Well," I replied. "At least they had crab."

As I looked into the eyes of my husband, who regularly told me with the voice of belief that I was beautiful, even when my face wore no makeup, and who never once complained when I didn't shave my legs, I thought, Sometimes we get what we never expected.

After a breakfast of pancakes the next morning, Ava and Alex watched cartoons with their great-grandmother while we waited for my mother's sister to arrive from Salem.

"Do I look like your Grammy?" she asked my children when she got there. I could hear hope in her voice.

"Sort-of," Ava replied.

"I think you look like Ava," my grandmother told her daughter. The round, blue eyes, I saw, were almost the same.

This time we trekked to the ocean with plastic shovels and pails. After stuffing sandwiches in our mouths, we raced across the sand to beat the tide to a favorite cove from my childhood that held the promise of agates. The walk to the lava rocks was longer than I had remembered. While I sifted through the pebbles regurgitated by the tide, I heard Poppy's voice. "That's just a common quartz," his words whispered through my mind as I gave the cloudy rocks back to the sea.

My grandmother, who had waited by the hillside near the parking lot, was impressed by the density of our pails when we returned. Later, as we sifted through our finds together on the glass of the table top, her words became her husband's. "Look at that. You found a rare one! It's a moss agate," she told me holding up a white rock veined with earth.

On our fourth day in Oregon, we packed lunches and my grandmother's walker into our rental SUV and headed south to the Oregon Seacoast Aquarium in Newport. Sleep deprivation and overwhelm had finally set in. Ava melted down in the car on the ride over. Alex, at the gift shop, while trying to decide what toy he could get with his $5 limit.

I too felt laden with emotion as I watched sea life trapped behind thick panes of glass. The sharks moved too slowly in the dim

266

water of their tank, and the giant crabs piled upon each other in a futile ladder to freedom.

When we reached the touch tanks, the density began to lift. My children, with sleeves rolled, squeezed their way into spots beside the open glass, and dipped their fingers into the water to pet the life that could feel open air but could not get away.

My husband and I greeted the next day with a run on the beach, leaving our children with my grandmother who was downstairs watching morning talk shows. Alex and Ava, piled on the futon upstairs, were happily glued to the treat of cable cartoons.

Running across the sand with Dave beside me, I wondered why I had waited until mid-week to join him in his morning jog. As we ran, my eyes wandered to the areas on the sand where rocks collected from the tide, stopping at intervals to pick up agates, bits of sea glass, and shells until my fists were full. My husband, beside me, laughed. "You just can't resist the urge, can you?"

We turned to run back the way we came, our bodies pressed against the current of the wind, while the sand slid beneath our feet. We ran until our bodies felt the test of endurance, and then, together, we stopped.

Later, we left my grandmother to relax with her crossword puzzles and talk shows while the four of us hiked a hidden trail through a temperate rainforest. Alone, in the woods, we snapped pictures of our family of four among the dripping moss. While we hiked the gradual incline, Ava and Alex laughed and argued, sliding ring pops on their fingers and singing through the sugar that spread a stain of blue around their lips.

At the end of the day, we met the out-going tide for one last search for agates. Again, the four of us were alone, the wind too fierce to tempt other hunters over the steep rocks that led to the cove. While the breeze tried to tip us into the sea, the four of us held hands, arms linked together to help balance feet, as we crossed over the cliffs of lava rocks. The wind, even stronger in the cove, shortened our stay, but the agates tumbled by the restless water soon filled the bottoms of our bags.

On our last full day on the coast, my grandmother suggested a drive to Taft to see the driftwood that piles up like petrified forests on the sand. While my grandmother found a log to sit on, blending the hues of her tan jacket and her white hair into the backdrop of decay and sand, Ava, Alex, Dave and I created castles. I captured the play of the sun upon the still water of the cove sprinkled with terns behind my children's smiling bodies, and tried not to think about tomorrow.

The next morning, we woke knowing we must soon leave a place we had all fallen in love with. My husband and I took pictures of the house we were renting, and the one next door, both for sale, in our need to believe that one day we might make summers on the Oregon coast an annual event. I smiled, marveling at how quickly my family had fallen in love with the state of my birth.

Irritation set in while I packed suitcases and emptied the refrigerator. I couldn't help thinking about what I would be leaving behind. After the trunk of the SUV was packed tight with our belongings, my husband suggested we stop along the seaside to take one more photograph of the ocean. With my mind already fixed on the trip ahead, I told him, "No, let's just start back east. We've got a long drive."

It did take a long time to get to Portland, the drive lengthened by the traffic that we couldn't seem to avoid. "You know," my grandmother told us. "Oregon is the number one tourist destination this summer."

On our way back to the city, to break up the drive, we stopped at the Evergreen Aviation & Space Museum in McMinnville. My grandmother decided to wait in the lobby, and while my son found heaven amid the myriad planes and rockets, I worried about time and his great-grandmother, sitting in wait. We still had another building to tour.

During the walk across the parking lot, we stopped at the car to dine on turkey and Tillamook cheddar sandwiches. After we were finished lunch, my grandmother pulled out her crossword saying, "Take your time. Don't worry about me," before we moved on to the next building of aeronautical wonders.

Back in Portland, we settled my exhausted grandmother into her condo and unloaded the extra groceries into her refrigerator and cabinets. Again, I found myself worrying about time.

"Why don't we take some pictures before we leave?" I told my grandmother. As Dave captured four generations minus one sitting on the sofa, I couldn't help but think about who was missing.

Moments later, I embraced my grandmother and felt the tug of separation. "We'll be back again soon," I told her, trying not to look at the veil of tears across her eyes. It was a promise I had every intention of keeping.

I called my father on my cell phone before we drove away. The family reunion he had been planning with my Aunt Linda did not begin until five o'clock, so, at only 3:00 p.m., we still had enough time to visit my uncle Robert in the assisted living facility near my grandmother's condo.

I had last seen Robert when I was, I think, younger than twelve. I remember him from my childhood as a quiet, but kind man who was not often around when I was at Grammie's house. When he was wheeled into the lobby of the assisted living facility, I recognized my uncle immediately. His large brown eyes and olive skin, inherited by his Croatian mother, seemed only more pronounced by the lines of age. On his head he wore a baseball cap, just like in my memories.

Robert smiled when he saw us, then looking at me, he asked, "What is your name?" Startled, I turned to my father, who had told me only that my uncle was looking forward to seeing us.

"This is my daughter, Alethea, Robert, and her family. You remember Alethea," he replied but, I was not sure.

My father then wheeled his brother outside to the garden. While my children explored the greenhouse filled with tomato plants, Robert tried to make sense of who we were. "What's your name?" he asked me again with eyes searching for recognition.

After discovering that my husband was a physician, Robert began telling him, in animated detail, about the summer of 1970 when he took a dive into the shallow water of a lake and hit his head on a cable on the way down. This memory of an event that occurred three years before my birth, I realized, would probably never leave him.

I took more pictures before we left Robert's home, this time with three generations descended from my father's side.

"What is your name again?" my uncle asked one last time before I kissed his cheek.

"Alethea," I whispered, wondering, as my lips touched his face, if he would remember me now.

On the drive to my aunt's, I checked my emotions, expecting at least a hint of anxiety, and found none. With my family beside me, I was ready for this reunion. When we pulled up to the curb near Linda's house, we were all eager to get out of the car.

It took me more time than I had expected to find recognition at my aunt's place, which was undergoing a renovation project that included a large addition and new landscaping. I found it later, as my daughter picked blueberries from the bushes in the backyard. My mind recalled a hillside of berries and a tree laden with cherries.

While my husband and I mingled with my family, Ava and Alex ate and played with their second-cousins. Together, they inhaled hotdogs and fruit picked by their own hands from the berry bushes in the yard, while the rest of us dined on barbecued meats and homemade tamales. Linda, who had once waitressed at Poncho's with Grammie, had made a dip from the restaurant's house recipe, and as the creamy mix of tomato and spices turned across my tongue, I thought of summers long past.

Too soon, the setting sun began to give way to the gray light of dusk, and I found myself gathering my children and husband in an effort to get us to bed for our early departure the next morning. As my father walked the four of us to our car, I could feel, already, our loss. After I buckled my son into his seat, I turned without hesitation to embrace the parent I had spent most of my life trying to forget.

"Goodbye, dad," I whispered into the cotton of his shirt.

My father's eyes, when he released me, held the same salty waters that were filling my own. I knew, this time for certain, he would miss me. And, I knew, I would miss him.

Acknowledgements

I would like to express a deep gratitude for all the teachers and companions in my life, many of whom appear as characters on the pages of this manuscript. I believe we agreed to embark on this journey together, and to have our lives intersect so that we could learn from each other. Although these lessons have not always been easy, their foundation is premised on a love that transcends this life-time. Through my own, deepest heartache I have found the place of beautiful healing. I have found my truth. I thank you for your role in this.

Thank you to my Goddard College advisers Kenny Fries, Rhana Reiko Rizzuto and, most especially, Jan Clausen for enabling this story of truth to start emerging onto the page. With infinite gratitude to Tara, Heidi and Larissa for their editorial work, support, and encouragement to bring my words to life. Tara, this is your story too, and your courage has helped me birth it.

To my other writing sisters, Carol, Jill, Jeanette, Elisabeth, Stacy, Karen and Sophia thank you for intersecting your journeys with mine, and giving me courage to write and share these words. To Sue, who has encouraged me to release the hold on this book with the offering, "if you feel it can help even one person, that is enough." A soul is healed by love, and I thank my many friends and fellow travelers on this journey of life.

I would like to express gratitude to my family who offered their memories, even when it was difficult, as well as their love and support. For some, the publication of this book comes with reluctance. I hope, one day, you are able to see the light of love within my words.

To my husband, son and daughter, and to Daisy, who has now passed over the rainbow bridge, but joins us often in spirit, there is a love and gratitude in my heart for you that cannot properly be expressed in words. You have shown me the true meaning of family.

Finally, thank you to the unseen, but felt, energy of Spirit that moves through my words.

I would like to acknowledge the *HerStories Project* and *Airplane Reading* for publishing earlier versions of pieces of writing that appear in this manuscript.

Memory does not necessarily define universal truth, but an individual's truth. I wrote this memoir through the filter of my memory and truth, except where I shared the memories of others. My truths and memories of events are my own, and do not necessarily reflect those of the characters in my story who shared these events. Most names and some defining characteristics have been changed to protect identities. It is not my wish to harm or offend any of the people who have shared a part of my life. I wrote my story to heal my truth, I offer it to you, my reader, so that you may use it to help find your own truth.

About the Author

ALETHEA KEHAS is a writer, poet, student of the mysteries, and owner of Inner Truth Healing. She lives in Bow, New Hampshire with her family of four humans plus four animal companions. Alethea believes that we are each on a journey to discover and live our soul's truth. Her healing work is devoted to helping people find their path to inner awareness. When she is able to, she escapes into the landscape in search of magic. For more information about Alethea, please visit her website: aletheakehas.com

52967781R00174

Made in the USA
San Bernardino, CA
02 September 2017